How to Get the Promotion You Want in 90 Days or Less:

A Step-by-Step Plan for Making It Happen

By: Lexi M. Schuh

How to Get the Promotion You Want in 90 Days or Less: A Step-by-Step Plan for Making it Happen

Copyright © 2009 Atlantic Publishing Group, Inc.
1405 SW 6th Avenue • Ocala, Florida 34471 • Phone 800-814-1132 • Fax 352-622-1875
Web site: www.atlantic-pub.com • E-mail: sales@atlantic-pub.com
SAN Number: 268-1250

No part of this publication may be reproduced, stored in a retrieval system, or transmitted in any form or by any means, electronic, mechanical, photocopying, recording, scanning, or otherwise, except as permitted under Section 107 or 108 of the 1976 United States Copyright Act, without the prior written permission of the Publisher. Requests to the Publisher for permission should be sent to Atlantic Publishing Group, Inc., 1405 SW 6th Avenue, Ocala, Florida 34471.

All trademarks, trade names, or logos mentioned or used are the property of their respective owners and are used only to directly describe the products being provided. Every effort has been made to properly capitalize, punctuate, identify and attribute trademarks and trade names to their respective owners, including the use of ® and ™ wherever possible and practical. Atlantic Publishing Group, Inc. is not a partner, affiliate, or licensee with the holders of said trademarks.
The Dale Carnegie Training program name and logo is a registered trademark and property of Dale Carnegie & Associates, Inc.
The Discovery Channel name and logo is a trademark and property of Discovery Communications, Inc.
The Simpsons name and logo is a trademark and property of Twentieth Century Fox Film Corporation.

ISBN-13: 978-1-60138-285-6   ISBN-10: 1-60138-285-5

Library of Congress Cataloging-in-Publication Data

Schuh, Lexi M., 1974-
    How to get the promotion you want in 90 days or less : a step-by-step plan for making it happen / by Lexi M. Schuh.
        p. cm.
    Includes bibliographical references and index.
    ISBN-13: 978-1-60138-285-6 (alk. paper)
    ISBN-10: 1-60138-285-5 (alk. paper)
    1. Promotions. 2. Career development. I. Title.
HF5549.5.P7S36 2009
650.14--dc22
                                    2008035553

LIMIT OF LIABILITY/DISCLAIMER OF WARRANTY: The publisher and the author make no representations or warranties with respect to the accuracy or completeness of the contents of this work and specifically disclaim all warranties, including without limitation warranties of fitness for a particular purpose. No warranty may be created or extended by sales or promotional materials. The advice and strategies contained herein may not be suitable for every situation. This work is sold with the understanding that the publisher is not engaged in rendering legal, accounting, or other professional services. If professional assistance is required, the services of a competent professional should be sought. Neither the publisher nor the author shall be liable for damages arising herefrom. The fact that an organization or Web site is referred to in this work as a citation and/or a potential source of further information does not mean that the author or the publisher endorses the information the organization or Web site may provide or recommendations it may make. Further, readers should be aware that Internet Web sites listed in this work may have changed or disappeared between when this work was written and when it is read.

Printed on Recycled Paper

BOOK MANAGER & EDITOR: Melissa Peterson • mpeterson@atlantic-pub.com
COVER DESIGNER: Shannon Preston
JACKET DESIGNER: Holly Marie Gibbs • hgibbs@atlantic-pub.com
Printed in the United States

We recently lost our beloved pet "Bear," who was not only our best and dearest friend but also the "Vice President of Sunshine" here at Atlantic Publishing. He did not receive a salary but worked tirelessly 24 hours a day to please his parents. Bear was a rescue dog that turned around and showered myself, my wife Sherri, his grandparents Jean, Bob and Nancy and every person and animal he met (maybe not rabbits) with friendship and love. He made a lot of people smile every day.

We wanted you to know that a portion of the profits of this book will be donated to The Humane Society of the United States. –Douglas & Sherri Brown

The human-animal bond is as old as human history. We cherish our animal companions for their unconditional affection and acceptance. We feel a thrill when we glimpse wild creatures in their natural habitat or in our own backyard.

Unfortunately, the human-animal bond has at times been weakened. Humans have exploited some animal species to the point of extinction.

The Humane Society of the United States makes a difference in the lives of animals here at home and worldwide. The HSUS is dedicated to creating a world where our relationship with animals is guided by compassion. We seek a truly humane society in which animals are respected for their intrinsic value, and where the human-animal bond is strong.

Want to help animals? We have plenty of suggestions. Adopt a pet from a local shelter, join The Humane Society and be a part of our work to help companion animals and wildlife. You will be funding our educational, legislative, investigative and outreach projects in the U.S. and across the globe.

Or perhaps you'd like to make a memorial donation in honor of a pet, friend or relative? You can through our Kindred Spirits program. And if you'd like to contribute in a more structured way, our Planned Giving Office has suggestions about estate planning, annuities, and even gifts of stock that avoid capital gains taxes.

Maybe you have land that you would like to preserve as a lasting habitat for wildlife. Our Wildlife Land Trust can help you. Perhaps the land you want to share is a backyard—that's enough. Our Urban Wildlife Sanctuary Program will show you how to create a habitat for your wild neighbors.

So you see, it's easy to help animals. And The HSUS is here to help.

THE HUMANE SOCIETY OF THE UNITED STATES

2100 L Street NW • Washington, DC 20037 • 202-452-1100
www.hsus.org

Author Dedication

This book is dedicated to my husband for his endless commitment and devotion to our family.

Contents

Foreword **11**

Introduction **15**

Chapter 1: Who Are You? **23**

Analyzing Yourself and Your Current Role................. 27

Overcoming a Negative Reputation............................ 29

What Are Peers in Your Office, Your Field, and the Workforce Doing? 31

Warding Off Feelings of Entitlement 32

Workable Deficiency.. 33

Capitalize on Your Strengths....................................... 35

Qualifications 37

Desires 38

Chapter 2: What Do You Want? **43**

Miswanting... 45

Work and Life Balance.. 48

Are You in the Right Field, Setting, and Company? ... 50

Your Boss Holds the Key 53

Goal-Setting... 56

The Peter Principle 59

Chapter 3: Seeking Opportunities — 63

Looking for Opportunities 66

Creating Opportunities 68

Honing Your Foresight 71

Become a Pro at Being Proactive 74

Chapter 4: Cleaning Up Your Job Performance — 79

Know Exactly What You Do...................................... 82

Continued Education and Ongoing Learning............. 84

Cultivating a Positive Attitude 89

Hours, Dedication, and Efficiency 91

Becoming a Problem Solver 94

Preparing to Pass the Torch 95

Chapter 5: Get Organized — 99

Defining Your Basic Needs 102

Time Management 104

Establishing Systems... 106

Structuring Your Workspace 109

Preparing Synopses of Projects,
Duties, and Achievements 111

Stress-Busting 113

Chapter 6: Brand yourself — 117

What Makes You "You" 119

Outside Opinions on You 121

How to Cultivate and Promote
Your Best Two Brand-able Traits 124

Appearances 127

Chapter 7: Communication — 131

Sending and Receiving Messages 134

Speaking 135

Writing 140

Context Messages 144

Chapter 8: Preparing Your Case — 151

What Have You Done? 153

Method of Preparation and Presentation 155

What Exactly Do You Want? 157

What Will You Settle For? 159

Coming Up with Preemptive Counterarguments 162

Expectations 164

Scheduling the Meeting... 165

Chapter 9: Employers, Bosses, Managers, and Supervisors — 169

Understanding Your Boss 172

The Skill of Making Your Boss Look Good 174

Traits Supervisors Look for
in Promotable Employees 178

What Days and Times of Day
Are Best to Ask for a Promotion 181

Chapter 10: Coworkers and Network Associates — 187

Conflict Management 190

Know the People Around You 193

Building Relationships 195

When to Lead 198

Networking 199

Mentors 201

Office Politics 202

Chapter 11: Integrity — 205

Honesty 208

Trust 211

Customer Service 213

Dependability 215

Loyalty 218

Sincerity 219

Character 222

Reputation 223

Chapter 12: The Big Day! — 227

Preparation 230

Practice 231

Conversation 233

Keeping Your Cool 234

Appearance 236

Chapter 13: Top Ten Reasons Promotions Are Denied — 243

Interference with Prescribed Hierarchical Protocol 246

No Money in the Budget 247

Hassle of Staff Changes 248

Bad Timing 248

The Employee's Attitude.. 249

No Room for Growth 251

Too Much Competition.. 252

Not a Team Player 253

Limited Evidence of Productivity 254

Just Not Right for the Requested Position 255

Chapter 14: What to Do After You Get the Promotion — 259

Chapter 15: Ongoing Preparation for the Next Rise — 267

Conclusion — 273

Bibliography — 277

Author Biography — 279

Index — 281

Foreword

With 15 years of managerial experience, I can tell you a common conundrum exists in many organizations. As an employee, you want responsibility, ownership, good compensation, and, therefore, job satisfaction. As a manager, you want smart, capable, and reliable people who can get their job done and allow you to focus on other facets of your own job and performance. Yet, this kind of synergistic relationship is a rarity in many places of work.

Why is it seemingly so difficult to make this beneficial match? There are myriad pitfalls preventing a mutually beneficial, successful placement of capable staff in key positions. As an employee, you may be in a job that you do not enjoy, and it shows. You may find yourself in a position you are just not good at, and you need to consider aligning your skills with a more relevant position. Too often, employees mismatch their perception of stellar performance with the actual needs and bias of their supervisor. When asked, your supervisor may have less-than-flattering comments about you or list some annoying traits of yours, whether deserved or not. If you find that you do not like to be assertive and proactive in your job duties, you may be shocked to realize it translates to your boss that you are somewhat unreliable. Often, you are a good but unrecognized employee. You may not know what steps you can take to have your performance acknowledged. The road to receiving the promotion you want and deserve can be fraught with peril. Over the years, in my work there has been no shortage of workplace circumstances from which to draw examples of "career-eliminating moves" or just career-stagnating moves by many employees.

More positively, I also reminisce about those "dream" employees, the ones you can rely on to take care of business in a happy and responsible manner. These are the ones for whom you enthusiastically answer "Yes!" when asked, "Would you hire this employee again?" Managers give promotions to those employees when they can, recognizing their stellar employee's success will make them successful too.

My relationship with the talented author of this book has blossomed outside our respective work experiences. Over the last 10 years, I have grown to love her brilliant mind. We have shared a fascination with the behavior of people and often share stories of the various workplace mishaps, blunders, success stories, and tales of either amazingly ridiculous or occasionally clever and efficient coworkers, bosses, and employees we have experienced on our respective paths.

Years of observation, experience, and research has led the author, Lexi M. Schuh, to a bright and talented examination of workplace pitfalls preventing you from achieving the job satisfaction you desire by becoming the employee every manager is salivating to hire. Her book, "How to Get the

Promotion You Want in 90 Days or Less: A Step-by-Step Plan for Making It Happen," is comprehensive yet simple in its elegant implementation. She has masterfully covered the successful traits and actions of a happy, motivated, productive employee. She does this while expertly guiding you away from the pitfalls and obstacles in your path to satisfaction, good compensation, workplace happiness, and the promotion you desire.

She has presented you with a weekly road map for success in a manner that allows you to move forward quickly and gives you tools you can start to implement immediately.

As a seasoned manager and employee myself, I can attest that the steps outlined in this book will work to help you find the success and happiness you desire and deserve. I would be glad to hire and place my trust in any person who exhibits the traits the author has outlined in this book. Good luck and best success!

Jennifer L. Dincola CPA, MBA

Currently Director of Finance for KDVR Fox 31 Television,

Jennifer L. Dincola has more than 20 years of high-level experience in executive, managerial, finance, and operating roles within broadcasting, advertising, high-tech international manufacturing, gaming, commercial services, and public accounting. Jennifer has held the positions of President and CEO of Newtek Strategies of Colorado, a subsidiary of Newtek Business Services, and as Chief Financial Officer and Chief Operating Officer at Thomas & Perkins Advertising, one of the largest full-service branding agencies in the Denver Metro area, with revenues over $40 million annually. Jennifer coauthored *The European Monetary Union: A Practical Guide for Business*, published by Carmel Produce of Israel, for worldwide corporate distribution.

Introduction

Work is called *work* for a reason. But heading into the workplace does not have to be a negative experience. Yet, according to a recent survey in *USA Today*, nine out of ten people feel unimportant in their jobs. One of the best predictors of employee satisfaction is feeling important at work, so it is puzzling why so many people accept feelings of insignificance and dissatisfaction. To find more happiness at work, all they need to do is claim it. To achieve the sense of accomplishment required for job satisfaction, you must create a pattern of positive, forward movement through your workplace experiences.

In 1999, almost a decade prior to the *USA Today* report, Richard B. Freeman and Joel Rogers co-authored the book "*What Workers Want.*" They reported similar findings of job dissatisfaction. In their research, which included the most comprehensive workplace study to be conducted since the 1970s, Freeman and Rogers discovered that workers wanted to feel as though they had a voice in their workplace. Without that sense of significance and importance, workers claimed dissatisfaction in their jobs. This sentiment mirrors the recent *USA Today* report, in which 90 percent of the interviewed workers revealed that feelings of unimportance and having no voice had caused them to feel dissatisfied in their work. Drastic changes to the workforce climate have transpired between the Freeman and Rogers study and the more recent *USA Today* report and, yet, workers are still claiming dissatisfaction for the same reasons. Only today they are complaining in greater numbers and doing so through more hours on the job.

When you consider that the average U.S. employee spends about 2,000 hours a year on the job, the idea that so many people have resigned themselves to accepting these dismal feelings of mediocrity, unhappiness, and unimportance during such a large share of their time seems ludicrous. Most people spend a far greater amount of time on the job than they do sleeping. Yet, no one would opt to spend the night on the front lawn in an uncomfortable pile of rocks when there is a perfectly inviting bed complete with springy mattress and 300-thread count sheets in their bedroom. Millions of workers accept the dissatisfying proposition of sleeping in the yard in agony even though there is a better option nearby. All they have to do is make a more comfortable bed. You make your bed, and then you lay in it.

Back in the day, when the worker bees of yore would grudgingly roll out of bed in the early morning and trudge to work to put in their requisite time, punching the clock in the morning and watching it all day before finally making their merciless escape at 5 p.m. on the dot, work dissatisfaction seemed the norm. Happiness and work were like oil and water. A symbiosis of the two did not exist. It was not even a part of the equation. People went to work because that is what you did. Times were different. In the 20th century, the body of literature documenting the problem of job dissatisfaction was just getting started. The term "job satisfaction" was in its infancy and had not yet made a significant impact on the general workforce. Work was what you did to make it to the weekend so you could finally relax and recuperate. You made it to Friday and got yourself all fixed up to get back to the treadmill on Monday.

Today, most people recognize the value of job satisfaction. With so many opportunities available in this ever-changing global economy, finding satisfaction at work is more possible than ever before. Part of the cause for change has been through the evolution of work as a concept. Work used to be something that you did to keep your idle hands and mind occupied and to provide shelter and food to one's self and family. Today, work is that and much more. The concept of work in the modern world brings up thoughts of self-expression, passion, goal achievement, strength utilization, and more. Work is not just about "bringing home the bacon" anymore. It is a main vehicle by which millions of people hope to find their true selves and gain personal satisfaction. If 90 percent of those people are resigning themselves to 2,000 hours a year of unhappiness instead, clearly they are not getting what they want out of the experience.

The ladder at work is meant to be climbed, to help each individual grow to his or her highest capacity, to feed the passions that burn inside of everyone, and to make work the ever-learning opportunity it can be. The ancient archetype of the hardened worker bee struggling to make it through the day needs to be put to rest. But the archetype, the burnt out treadmill bee, is not right either. In place of these two disappointing work models comes the new, improved image: the sprite, eager worker bee who loves the job and is ready to work. This new ideal is achievable for anyone who is willing to put in the time, effort, and introspection to make it happen.

So, how do you move from that sad, little bored or overworked bee to the vibrant one sizzling with the desire to grow? And how can you maximize that desire to thrust forward and avoid typical mistakes in the process? The answer is found in the step-by-step plan outlined in this book. You can take yourself from simply having the desire for advancement to knowing how to put a plan into action and nab the promotion you want. If you are prepared to put in 90 days of effort toward this goal, you will get results.

Starting the first week you put this plan into action, you will begin a journey toward understanding who you are, why you have not yet earned the promotion you feel you deserve, and how you can actively take steps toward achieving your goals. Every week for 12 weeks, you will tackle a new chapter and that week's target area with objectives to guide you. Additionally, you will participate in self-exploration exercises to further confirm what steps you should be taking to reach your goals and to prevent you from making the mistakes that have held other people back from their goals. You will find assistance through descriptions of the possible pitfalls that might hold you back. Case studies, based on the knowledge and real-life experiences of top-hiring managers and professionals, will provide further evidence throughout this book to guide you in your pursuit.

At the end of the 12-week program, you will follow up on all you have learned and discover how you can further put your new knowledge into practice through the guidance of the three final chapters. Each of these chapters have a specific focus that will help you to avoid any final mistakes as you carry through to requesting your promotion and after you have attained what you have desired. In these final chapters you will learn the most often-cited reasons why promotions are denied, how you can maintain the success you have achieved in winning your promotion, and what you should do to start preparing yourself for your next eventual promotion.

Specifically, you will learn such things as:

- How to set appropriate and attainable goals

- How to seek and create opportunities for professional growth

- How to become better organized

- How to successfully and memorably brand yourself

- How to communicate effectively in all facets of your professional life

- How to cultivate and preserve your integrity

- How to prepare yourself for the meeting to discuss your potential promotion

Taking on the challenge of trying to get a promotion is like accepting a whole new job on top of your current one. In addition to keeping up with the duties of the job you already have, you will be assigning yourself the tasks of better keeping up with your existing duties in addition to putting in the work toward grooming yourself for the promotion you will soon earn — with *"earn"* being the operative word.

Many people mistakenly assume they have earned rights to a promotion through tending to the tasks of their present position. This is simply not true. Most workplace organizations adhere to the basic rules of annual salary adjustments contingent on typical price of living increases. This means that for every year you give to your employer, you may anticipate a pay increase of roughly 3 to 7 percent. Additionally, some workplace organizations also incorporate time- and productivity-relevant patterns according to what an employee can expect to move up within the organization. However, nobody should assume they will have specifically earned access to greater rewards and higher positions for doing the job they are being paid to do.

If you hope to earn a promotion, you must recognize that the great work you have put into your present position and the accomplishments you have attained therein are somewhat irrelevant to this goal. All that you have achieved thus far provides merely an indication to your boss that you have a potential future within the organization. Certainly, if you have maintained a positive work history so far, you will be more likely to start your promotion negotiations on a good foot. However, you should not assume you are owed the opportunity for growth and greater rewards simply because you have put in the time or kept up with the demands of your job.

There are many different points of view relevant to the reality that past work performance and future potential are only correlative and not directly cause-and-effect. For some people, knowing they are off to a fresh start will be comforting. Perhaps these individuals may have a sketchy work history or recognize that they have not done as good a job at work as they could have. Other people may find it unjust that the quality work they have given to the job so far does not automatically give them access to promotions. Yet, there is definitely a distinction between earning a promotion because an individual has been doing his or her job well and earning a promotion because the employee has put in the effort to specifically attain the goal of moving up in the organization. Whatever standpoint you come from as you begin this journey, begin your efforts with the comforting knowledge that you can achieve your goal of getting a promotion if you put in the work.

Treat this book as your week-to-week guide. Do not overwhelm yourself by digesting the whole thing at once. You will be busy enough as it is, doing the job you have already plus taking actions to procure the next phase of your career. Some weeks will be more challenging than others, depending on your strengths, weaknesses, and the ebbs and flows of life, but be wary of those weeks that seem like a breeze. It is often overconfidence in one's strengths that hinders a person's ability to tune up the whole package.

Sometimes, the areas in which you are highly adept but could still use a little work are the areas that hold you back from reaching the next level. The smartest people in the world are those who know their strengths and weaknesses, but continuously work toward gaining the knowledge and skills they know are missing. Through the weeks ahead, you will become attuned to your strengths so you can work them to your best advantage. You will come to terms with your weaknesses to determine how they have held you back and what you can do to overcome their detriment.

To start on this journey of self-understanding and growth, the first step is to figure out who you are exactly. In this first week of the program, you will be exploring the big world of you. What makes you tick? What are your strengths and weaknesses? Why have you chosen the job you are in, and how can you ensure you are prepared for a promotion to take your work life up to the next step? What makes you unique, and why do you deserve a promotion? And, better yet, what can you do to ensure you will be able to keep up with the demands of the promotion?

CHAPTER 1

Who Are You?

This week's checklist:

- Think about the positive traits in your nonwork life. Do you apply those traits to your work success? If not, could you be channeling those characteristics to find more success at work?

- Focus on what can be improved, and depend on your strengths.

- Ask your close friends about their work experiences. Do they feel they are paid enough, are they happy in their jobs, and how do they plan to grow at work? Learning from other people will give you a new perspective.

- Read the business section of your newspaper or a business news Web site at least once this week. Learning more about the workforce in the broad sense will help you to understand the microcosm of your workplace.

- Read at least one workplace-related Internet blog this week. Reading the complaints and comments of other people in the workforce will show you how common feelings of entitlement are and, likely, how positive your workplace seems in comparison.

Before embarking on this journey toward earning a promotion, you are going to have to practice some heavy-duty tough love — on yourself. You will need to rise up to the challenge of being the best you can be, but first you must confront yourself with some beat-yourself-to-a-pulp attacks on your personality. Your reality at work is based on how you are presenting yourself, what special talents you are using, and how other people perceive you. You may be the smartest, most talented person around, but if you are not demonstrating that at work, then it is not your workplace reality. Looking at yourself so closely that you see how others are seeing you may be uncomfortable, but it is the only way to confront the reality of who you are currently at work so you may transform yourself into who you want to be.

Many people mistakenly assume they deserve a promotion simply for doing their job satisfactorily for a good length of time. Maybe when you were in grade school you became accustomed to earning a ribbon on Field Day just for showing up. Real life does not and should not work that way. You accepted the role of your current job and you are being paid to do that job, so adhering to that agreement between you and your employer does not justify a blue ribbon. Winning the race through hard work, intelligence, and perseverance, however, does justify a reward.

In today's workforce, the younger workers, 18 to 24, cite the most dissatisfaction at work, while the older workers, aged

44 to 62, claim the most satisfaction. Analysts suggest that the reason the younger segment, the Y Generation, are so displeased at work has less to do with the reality of their jobs and more to do with unfilled expectations common to their cohorts. The older segment, the Baby Boomers, have been dubbed the "Me Generation." Yet, it is more often the younger workers whose dissatisfaction at work indicates a tendency to focus on their own perceived reality in the workforce rather than the potential opportunities available to them.

Your workplace does not need to be unsatisfying. The organization in which you work runs on people power, and, as such, your employer wants you to succeed because he or she wants the organization to succeed. Therefore, the dissatisfaction you feel at work has less to do with the reality of the potential growth available to you and more to do with how you are holding yourself back from seizing those opportunities. The organization needs smart, qualified, hard workers. If you are not given opportunities to show you have what they want, there is a discrepancy between your perceived reality according to your supervisors and your actual experience. To understand how different your perceived reality is from your actuality, you must figure out who you are according to what you are portraying and who you are in truth.

Determining who you are is the existential question that plagues just about everyone through the course of his or her whole life. People spend millions of dollars on therapy, self-help books, and counseling to answer the questions of their own existence and still come back dissatisfied. Seeking answers to explain why you are a certain way and what will satisfy you is a process in which you will be involved for the rest of your days. Although you can never have full knowledge of yourself (your subconscious ensures that you will not), coming to terms with your basic essence requires a lifetime commitment to ongoing learning and will help you in the process of better understanding yourself for the rest of your days.

If you want to earn a promotion, you must make an effort to honestly examine what kind of person you are in all aspects of your life. The type of person you are in social settings outside work matters in the workplace even when you are not socializing. Such things as the habits, hobbies, exercise tendencies, energy level, and outlook you have regarding personal relationships make up who you are as a person. Although those characteristics may not apply to your job, they are all still components of you. Therefore, those components and more affect who you are and will help you to understand who you are in the workplace.

In addition to all the aspects of your personality that you demonstrate during your off-work hours, you also have an isolated work personality to analyze. You have tendencies, traits, and talents that you apply only at work. You have cultivated these tendencies, traits, and talents through your life experiences and have honed them all on the job.

Another important step in understanding yourself is in examination of the negative tendencies of your behavior. Understanding these parts of your personality is essential for consistent self-improvement. You may learn as much about yourself through other people's perceptions of your negative behavior as you will from dissecting them yourself.

Comparing yourself to other people can be an exercise in self-defeating futility. There will always be someone who is more attractive, more talented, or smarter. Yet, comparing yourself as a worker to others in the workforce may give you a better understanding of your market value and help you to determine what you could be entitled to in your workplace. This, of course, should not be confused with the concept of feelings of misplaced entitlement but rather is meant in reference to entitlements you specifically earn.

Successfully and thoroughly analyzing who you are is a vital component of putting together your promotion plan. Understanding how you function in life and in the workplace will help you to use and hone your assets, improve your shortfalls, and guide your goals. First, you need to explore who you are, both during your off-hours and at work, to assess how good a job you are doing at the position you currently hold. Understanding these aspects of yourself will help you to successfully and efficiently move forward.

Analyzing Yourself and Your Current Role

You have many facets to your personality. You have behaviors specific to work, behaviors specific to personal life, and behaviors specific to the different settings in both your work and personal life. Although these different behaviors are typical to each specific environment, you use them across your environments as well. Also, these facets of you matter, because they are still a part of you, even when you are not channeling them.

Any positive trait that is a part of a person's off-hours personality can be successfully used in his or her workplace. For example, an individual who is loyal to another individual in a nonwork, interpersonal relationship possesses a trait that could be useful in his or her workplace. Being loyal to an organization is a lot like being loyal to a person, effecting positive results in both scenarios. A person who is nurturing in relationships away from work can channel that tendency and use it in the workplace. Being able to tend to others' needs is an extremely marketable commodity in workplace settings.

To understand who you are at work, examine your personality on the job, but also think about who you are away from work. You may find that you have not been tapping into some of your best traits.

In addition to how you function as an individual, how you function as a member of groups is just as important to understanding who you are. People function in groups in spite of but also because of their differences. Groups of people, such as members of a neighborhood community, may not always get along because they function so differently, but it is that differentiation of personalities that contributes to the unified goals. You have specific characteristics that make you a necessary component to your community or groups. Understanding what helps you function in your communities away from work will help you understand what will help you to function in your work communities.

The experiences in your life have also served to carve out the path you are on and how successfully you function in organized settings. Your childhood, teen years, college and young-adult years, and adult-life experiences have contributed to your uniqueness. Think about your personal history and how your experiences have shaped the person you are and how you conduct yourself in group settings. Consider, for example, the differences between your personality away from work and the characteristics of your work personality. If you function differently in those group settings, imagine how you can apply the successes you have found in outside groups to those work settings in which you feel unsuccessful.

One of the most important aspects of your work personality to consider is your attitude. Much of your individual and group successes are contingent on you having a positive attitude. A positive attitude is integral to other people's perceptions of you. Most of your success at work can be directly attributed to how others perceive your attitude. When you demonstrate a positive attitude, you will tend to perform more successfully as well as be given more opportunities by supervisors who notice your positive attitude. Top executives consistently name a positive and likeable attitude as the most important factor for hiring and promoting an employee.

When you prepare yourself for work in the morning, are you looking forward to the day's work, or do you look in the mirror and see a downtrodden worker bee who is just heading into work because "that is what you do"?

Sure, actual success on the job is important for a positive perception, but your accomplishments are not what walk into the boss's office — you are. Whom would you rather keep around: a complaining whiner who acts as though he or she is above the minutiae of the job or an individual who is always willing to help, has enthusiasm for the job, and understands there is always more to be learned?

Ask yourself:
- Am I eager to learn something new every day?
- Do I practice an outstanding work ethic every day?

- Do I show respect for other people's experience?
- Am I proactive in seeking out ways to go above and beyond my assigned duties?

If you answer no to any of these questions, you may need to do a little reputation cleanup.

People will be forgiving of your mistakes if you take responsibility for your own actions. If you have made the mistake of sporting a bad attitude, own up to it now. Leave that attitude at your front door and do not look back. Sometimes, though, that is easier said than done. The easiest way to overcome a negative reputation is to replace it with a positive one.

Overcoming a Negative Reputation

Based on what you have learned about yourself, you should have a good idea of what sort of attitude ailments need adjusting. Next, you need to kick those bad habits. One technique to try is finding an alternate behavior to replace a bad habit. Consider an individual who wants to quit smoking. Every time he longs for a drag, he chooses an icy glass of water instead. Pay attention to every action you perform at work this week. If you find yourself bristling at a veteran's constructive criticism (taking a puff of your cigarette), instead correct yourself by seeking out a learning opportunity (grab a glass of water) to make up for that bad behavior. In this instance you might choose to consider the advice and show appreciation, rather than choose to be insulted.

During the process of cleaning up your reputation, you will likely begin to pay closer attention to what everyone else is up to. It is only natural to compare yourself to other people, especially in a time of deep personal reflection. Do not shy away from that tendency. Use it to your advantage. Instead of getting frustrated when other people seem to be having an easier time than you, recognize that everyone struggles with insecurities and bad habits. You may not always see how they struggle — and that may drive you to compete against them and perhaps even play dirty — but other successful people are not your enemy. Recent research suggests it is more beneficial to work well with others than subscribe to the philosophy that nice guys finish last.

According to a Harvard study published in 2008, research shows you do not have to be bad to get ahead. Apparently, nice guys finish first, not last. Study coauthors Martin Nowack and David Rand determined that punishing others and inciting conflict puts people at a disadvantage. In the competitive games they set up for their experiment, the individuals who had fewer incidences of resorting to punishing behaviors, penalizing other participants with a "costly punishment" monetary charge, were more likely to be the victors. Conversely, the participants who enlisted the most incidences of punishing behaviors were more frequently the losers.

Instead of comparing yourself to others and seeing their success as a reason to punish them and hold yourself back, use other people as resources. Learn from your peers, and use that information to escalate your own career.

What Are Peers in Your Office, Your Field, and the Workforce Doing?

It seems simple enough to try to be the best "you" that you can be, but, just as your supervisors use the yardstick of your peers to gauge where you stand in the lineup, you will need to learn how to use that yardstick, too.

Look around your office. What are your peers doing? What do they do well? What do they do poorly? Who among them do you think will succeed? These people are your competition, but they are also people from whom you can learn. Even those individuals whom you do not personally like will possess characteristics from which you can learn. In taking the time to analyze other people's strengths and weaknesses, you will learn more about your own strengths and weaknesses by comparison and determine how you can improve.

Use your perceptions of what everyone else is doing to improve what you are doing. You do not need to adopt their best traits, but you can take positive lessons from both the high-performing individuals and those who are not as successful. From those whom you admire or who are functioning well, learn their techniques. Pay attention to what less- successful individuals are doing to learn what not to do.

Even though the job market is full of many different and new opportunities, you cannot bank on that expansiveness. The economy changes rapidly, and recent decreases in job departures indicate that job security could soon go into a tailspin. The economy is mercurial and, according to the Bureau of Labor Statistics, incidents of voluntary job departure decreased by 50 percent from 2006 to 2008. An ever-changing economy and evidence of higher retention in presently occupied positions indicates that job security and availability is precarious. As unique as you may be, what makes you think you are entitled to not only to keep your job, but also to continue to rise up the ranks?

Warding Off Feelings of Entitlement

Arguably one of the worst traits to come from recent generations is the pompous feeling of entitlement. Perhaps this attitude is due to all those ribbons and pats on the back for every meaningless action in school. Wherever this trend is coming from, do not fall into its trap. Do not become one of the many people who believe they are entitled to only the best simply for being alive. Earn your rewards through old-fashioned hard work, even if you see other people lazily taking advantage of loopholes that may get them rewarded more quickly. They will learn nothing through that path while you will always be growing and improving.

The old-school model of the workplace was designed so employees were rewarded for putting in their time and sticking with it. An old-school worker could hope to move up three levels maximum in the workplace — and that was through a lifetime of devotion and servitude to one company.

These days, workplace hierarchies run a little differently. Workers should not expect they will be rewarded simply for putting in their time — even if it is decades of committed work. After all, many other employees are putting in their time, too. Competition is stiffer than ever, so although the economy is full of many exciting opportunities, there are fewer high-level slots to fill. This is due to down-sizing and the acceleration of job loss during the economic crisis that began in 2008.

With more competition, fewer high-level slots to fill, and a hierarchy that does not necessarily reward time invested, no one is entitled to anything other than his or her prescribed paycheck and allotted days off. So get it out of your head that you are entitled to anything other than what the rest of the individuals at your current level are getting. Sure, you have your own unique characteristics and talents, but so do they. Promotion hierarchies are driven by production, perceptions of production, and perceptions of you. To show your top-dog status, you need to stand out from the pack.

Just as it is wise to know what you are good at, understanding where you have room for improvement is also a part of knowing who you are. Plus, how else will you grow if you do not tackle your workable deficiencies? Mr. Rogers may have convinced you that you were special just as you are, but there should be someone else in your life who might be a bit more honest. Ask a trusted, no-holds-barred friend to name three things he or she perceives to be your workable deficiencies. Do not press further for a discussion and do not blame the messenger for doing you this favor. Know that it is all about perceptions anyway. Grab a hold of one of those workable deficiencies and actively seek to improve — even if you feel you are special just as you are.

Workable Deficiency

Despite your valuable assets, you will have weaknesses. Even the most well-rounded individuals cannot be expected to master all capabilities. For example, an individual who is excellent at math may not have a wonderful singing voice. As hard as he or she works to improve that skill, that person will still never be made into a natural-born singer. Instead of focusing on the deficiencies that cannot be changed, pay attention to the hidden talents of your workable deficiencies.

No one is entitled to anything in this world. Everything is up to you and your ability to earn rewards for good behavior — remembering that sometimes, like in the case of a promotion, the reward may come in the form of more work. As you determine how you will earn your rewards, know that one of the best things you can do for yourself and your career is to capitalize on your strengths.

CASE STUDY: JENNIFER DINCOLA

Jennifer Dincola

Director of Finance

Fox 31 KDVR, Colorado

Recently, a collection of outside assessors were brought in for standard accounting and records examinations. The main group consisted of three staff members fresh out of college. As the audit wore on, my boss and I became increasingly dumbfounded at the way this group was operating. When my boss and I were starting out, we tirelessly threw ourselves into the hard work to demonstrate how smart and professional we were. This group was the exact opposite. They were full of inane questions and utterly lazy behavior. To get them to complete simple tasks they wanted to put off on me, I had to treat them as I do my children when they are trying to get me to do their homework for them by saying, "Well, I suggest you take it back to your office and spend a little time with it."

After watching this kind of behavior for a couple weeks and marveling that this was the best and the brightest the universities are putting out these days, I finally decided that when my children tell me they are the only ones of their friends who have to do chores and pay for their own things, they are not exaggerating. I started to believe that we've put out an entire generation of people who have no interest in working hard.

And then — a bright spot! A new young intern, Chris, showed up. He was eager, positive, optimistic, well-dressed, a pleasure to talk to, and polite. He wanted to learn as much as he could, was careful not to get in the way, and recognized the value of hard work and résumé building. My faith in the next generation had been restored.

Capitalize on Your Strengths

According to a recent survey, only one in ten people says he or she capitalizes on personal strengths at work. The best way to feel important and, thus satisfied, at work is to know you are putting your talents to good use. It is no wonder workers are so dissatisfied on the job — only 10 percent of workers are using the best parts of themselves. Workers can complete task after task, but if they know their strengths are not being used to full capacity, they are regularly neglecting a part of themselves.

You chose your profession for a reason — likely because you showed talents for the main components of your job. Get back to the root of what first attracted you to your work, what you are good at, and what you enjoy about it. These are your strengths. Reveling in them and using them to their full capacity will help you to enjoy your work and feel successful. When you use your strengths, you feel more confident. This is because even if you do not recognize it consciously, you need regular reinforcement of what makes you a unique and capable human being. Most jobs require that the worker wear many hats — some of which are ill-fitting. Your job is likely filled with an assortment of tasks that simply have to get done but which you are not as excited to do or which you feel you are not completely capable of doing.

When you remind yourself of your strengths, you can further capitalize on them by exploring new ways to use them to complete those other tasks that weigh you down.

The first step to capitalizing on your strengths happens when you refocus on your favorite parts of the job. Remind yourself why you got into this line of work and what you enjoy about it. For example, if you got into social services because you enjoy helping people and have a talent for empathy, use the strength of your empathetic nature every chance you get. Use it when you are working with clients, use it when you are dealing with coworkers, and use it when you are looking for ways in which you can help the organization — use your strengths at every opportunity. You will feel yourself getting stronger and more content, and, at the same time, a natural offshoot will be growth in your career.

If you have forgotten what your strengths are, which can happen when you get lost in the minutiae of your regular work duties, keep a list this week of everything that makes you feel happy at work. The things that bring us happiness at work are the things that make us feel competent and successful. Sometimes you will rediscover your strengths in things unrelated to the details of your job. Pay attention to how you successfully manage conflict, for example, to be reminded of your excellent problem solving and people skills.

When you remind yourself what your strengths are, think up some new ways to use those strengths to tackle those tasks that ordinarily weigh you down. For example, although you may not enjoy or have a talent for telephone-based customer service, use your strong written communication skills to control that facet of your work. By being creative in management of your work tasks and using your strengths to your best advantage, you will find more satisfaction and success at work.

Being reminded of your strengths and putting them to good use will feel good, but this sort of introspection does not come easy. All of it takes hard work. But putting your strengths in the forefront of your qualifications and dismissing the unchangeable deficiencies that you have used as an excuse to hold you back will leave more room for you to focus on honing your qualifications. You can and should always actively improve your professional qualifications. If you do not, you may get left behind or overlooked.

Qualifications

You must have some qualifications if you got the job you are in, but, to succeed and keep growing professionally, you need to find ways to continually expand on your bank of knowledge, skill set, professional training, and education.

Having an undergraduate degree is commonplace these days. Many equate it to a high school-level education in part because, although it used to be a more exclusive club, these days access to college is much easier. Funding options are available. Evening, weekend, and online courses allow more flexibility. Plus, more people place the expectation of college on our youth. It used to be that people could climb up the corporate ladder despite not having a college degree if they put in hard work and had exceptional intelligence. But today it is becoming harder to find those opportunities because organization heads will often see a huge flag if an individual has not finished college. Studies show that hiring personnel do not care so much what field a potential employee graduated in; they simply care you have finished. Of course this opinion depends on the person and position. Ask yourself if your higher education background is enough for you, your field, the position you are in, and the positions you want to be in, and make changes as needed.

Not all fields, of course, require a college degree, although it is rare for a college degree not to be perceived as an asset in any field. College or no college, lifelong learning through consistent efforts in personal growth is a must. This can come in the form of official and unofficial training courses, seminars, professional organization memberships, and professional journal subscriptions. Additionally, keeping attuned to the world at large and changes in it that are relevant to your field, organization, and community through daily readings of current-event media is a casual but still important way in which you can tend to your ongoing education. Ensure that you keep yourself abreast of important news in your field and the world.

Keeping your skill set sharp should be a regular part of your job. Many people seem to forget this. You were hired with a specific set of skills, so you must ensure that you keep them honed. Avoid such things as consistently cutting corners, outsourcing tasks to underlings, and neglecting duties in your line of work. Through these acts, you may not be keeping your skill set as razor sharp as you should. For instance, perhaps you have been less concerned about your writing skills because you rarely have to communicate this way. When you do not practice them, skills can become stagnant. If, as in this example, you neglect your writing skills and one day are faced with an opportunity in upper management, you do not want your memos to look as if they were written by a third-grader.

Your qualifications are what will get you the upward momentum you desire at work, but what drives that desire?

Desires

Discussing the idea of desires in the realm of work promotion goals may, to some, seem arbitrary and unconnected. After all, the concept of desire is more commonly perceived in alliance with pleasures such as sex and food cravings, rather than the more staid desires such as gaining leverage at work. But in the long run your desires to grow personally and professionally are at least as strong if not stronger than your fleeting desires to gorge on pizza. You may feel, say around lunch time, that your greatest desire is to dig into a cheeseburger, but surely your ongoing desire to get ahead at work has more relevance to the rational choices your brain makes on a regular basis. So, then, how are your work-related desires being formed and fulfilled in the course of your professional life?

Desires can be filed into two categories: terminal and instrumental. A terminal desire is representative of a desire alone. These, then, are aided by instrumental desires, those that contribute to attaining the terminal desire. Relative to earning a promotion, the award of the promotion itself is not the likely terminal desire. The terminal desire, what you ultimately hope to gain through fulfilling the desire to earn a promotion, is likely along the lines of wealth, power, or a more specific desire such as owning a high-priced item. The instrumental desires that will lead to fulfillment of your terminal desire, then, will include such things as doing your current job well, forging a better relationship with your boss, and determining your value on the market. These instrumental desires will, then, chain up to the broader desire of why you want to get a promotion. To understand and control your desire to earn a promotion, you will find it beneficial to decipher why this particular desire has become important to you.

Ask yourself what terminal desire led you to your instrumental desire of wanting to earn a promotion.

More money might be an obvious answer, but financial wealth does not directly correlate with a hedonic outcome. Nor does the desire to have more power or to have an impressive title or even to own a luxury automobile. What you believe you desire is often in direct correlation to what those around you want or dictate you should want. In this case, "those around you" refers to a culture that equates happiness with money, power, and materialism. In this week of self-reflection, reconsider the rationale for this desire of earning a promotion. Fulfilling a terminal desire that is driven by cues from culture can be surprisingly unsatisfying. Learning what terminal desire will satisfy you from the inside out and in the long term will help you to gain control over the chain of other instrumental desires intermeshed with the desire to earn a promotion.

Through this chapter on introspection you have cultivated a better idea of who you are in your workplace and who you are in life. Become the person who has a positive attitude and recognizes that there is always room for growth. Do not become the rainbow-ribbon wearer who mistakenly believes he or she should be rewarded simply for showing up. Determine where you stack up in the lineup of your peers so that you can figure out and then improve on your workable deficiencies and learn how to accentuate your strengths.

Coming to terms with your workable deficiencies can be difficult, but it is a necessary step toward self-actualization. You cannot improve if you do not take that cold, hard, honest look in the mirror and admit what can be improved. Do not focus on the weaknesses that cannot be changed into strengths. As you critically assess your deficiencies, at least you will have the buffer of acknowledging your strengths.

The work you have done to change your reality will benefit you through the rest of your career. It is an ongoing process, though, as you will constantly continue to change. The world, the workforce, your organization, and other people are always changing, too. Be prepared to actively continue improving yourself according to how the rest of the world is changing as well. Even though you have come closer to figuring out who you are, you must ensure that you do not let yourself become stagnant in your growth. Always be prepared to learn new skills and step into new opportunities.

After you have completed the process of facing your weaknesses and reveling in your strengths, you will have a better understanding of who you are and how to cultivate more flattering perceptions of you. Next, it is time to determine how to use your new actuality and determine what you want out of your job.

Possible Pitfalls:

- Watch out for those creeping feelings of entitlement.

- Do not miss out on the opportunity to translate your positive nonwork attributes to your workplace setting.

- Explore your desires fully. Consider all the instrumental desires that lead to a terminal desire. Just because you want it does not mean you need it.

- Know that those things you think you are not good at may be hidden talents you have never fully explored.

- Look at what is missing from your qualifications, and do something now to fix the problem.

CHAPTER 2

What Do You Want?

This week's checklist:

- Research current job statistics to discover what others in your field or with your qualifications and experience are earning.

- Practice goal-setting. Write down five goals at the start of this week that you will complete by the end of the week.

- Read your organization's employee handbook or discuss your office's protocol with an employee who has the information, such as someone in human resources, to understand any nuances of the promotion process.

- Read an article, journal, or book related to your work.

- Make a list of all the important and time-consuming aspects of your life and number them in basic order of priority. For example, some things that may be on your list will be family, work, exercise, home repair, and travel.

After you have analyzed who you are in the workplace, it is time to figure out what you want. Some people may think they want a promotion, but what they want is more money and perks — not necessarily the greater responsibility that may come with it. Or, they may be one of the estimated 85 percent of American workers who claim they are unhappy at work and, therefore, are looking for something tangible to appease that unhappiness. If you have bothered to buy a book about earning a promotion and are taking the time to enact a plan toward earning a promotion, chances are you do not just expect everything to be handed to you through no work of your own.

Where do you see this relationship with your workplace going? Do you just want some change — something to tide you over for a while because you have been feeling slightly disenchanted or bored in your current position? Are you anticipating a complete skyscraping climb up the work ladder because you feel you are ready to go full gusto? Your organization may have an established protocol that will dictate how far you may move up the ladder, so that is a consideration, or you may have a strict vision of what your climb up should look like. However your rise unfolds, putting your goals in perspective is as important to your success as enacting your plan toward achieving them. Planning for and achieving self-defined success at work is what will make you happy at work. More money, power, and perks may be part of it, but it is the feeling of success that will create your satisfaction.

Many things have contributed to your goal of wanting a promotion, and many more things affect the specifics of what you want in your promotion and how you will create your plan to attain it. In this process, you will discover that some of what you thought you wanted from your promotion will turn out to be misguided desires. You will learn that you do not need certain things to satisfy you. For example, you may believe that you want a specific monetary raise but find you are satisfied with a smaller raise and the ability to work from home two days a month. Although your original desire may have been to earn a grander title, you may discover what you need is a better balance between work and home life. In the beginning of this journey you might have thought your company was the problem, but along the way you learned that you like your company but not the section in which you work. You may determine that all you have been missing was a clear set of goals and that the walls you were hitting were attributable to your lack of a road map. This and more will be examined in this chapter.

So what do you want out of your job? To explore this question, first examine why it is that you have decided you want it.

Miswanting

Although the Rolling Stones suggested the problem with desire is that you "can't always get what you want," a pair of U.S. psychologists, Daniel Gilbert and Timothy Wilson, begged to differ in a 2001 book in which they coined the term "miswant." According to Gilbert and Wilson, the conundrum of human beings is not that we cannot get what we want; it is that we do not know what we want. We miswant things that we believe will make us happy but, once attained, still do not fill the cravings inside us.

The truth of miswanting is apparent in the quenching of even the most minor of desires. Consider an item you once coveted and then saved up to finally purchase. At first, you may have felt happy at getting what you wanted. You desired the item and, immediately upon purchasing, it may have felt a cool rush of ecstasy at having attained said item. But did getting what you thought you wanted have any real, lasting impact of happiness? Was the happiness received in proportion to the expectation built up around the want? Also, how long did it take for you to simply accept this once strongly desired object as another mediocre component of your series of belongings? It is rare that what you think you want coincides with what ends up satisfying you the most.

In terms of your career aspirations, consider what possible miswants have been guiding your goals. Chapter 1 addressed the outside influences that subconsciously steer your choices. Desires often have more to do with earning rights to what society indicates you should want, rather than what you would want if left to your own design of a happy life. According to research, human beings are terrible at predicting what personal designs for a happy life would look like because miswants consistently interfere with any ability to find happiness.

Why have you set these goals for yourself at work? Movies will portray financial wealth and impressive work titles as the recipe for success and happiness, even as celebrity news provides perfect counterargument against those claims. This is not to suggest there is anything wrong with wanting these things of their own merit. Having more money, for instance, surely can be a comfort. But the quandary in getting what you want in terms of a resource such as money is that you then get used to that new level of attainment and, guess what, you want even more. It is an ongoing cycle of partially filled desires. This particular recipe for happiness is an uneasy one, for the list of ingredients is always changing, fluctuating in required measurements, causing the chef frustrations at never finishing her creation.

Your reasons for desiring what you desire are your own and, at that, not open to the judgment of others. If you want more money, for instance, because you desire a red sports car, that is your desire to own — no defense necessary. If you want a higher title at work because your college roommate brags about her impressive résumé, then you recognize how minor jealousies can inspire us. The point is to not ignore your desires. Want what you want, but get to the root of how the miswants may eventually catch up with you. Money, power, and socially perceived statuses of success are rarely components in the recipe for long-term happiness. A good example of this is in the modern-day trend of neglect to a comfortable work and life balance.

Work and Life Balance

For many people, the concept of work and life balance has gone wayward thanks to the modern-day pressures to live a fast lifestyle. Both men and women have fallen victim to this trap.

Since women were better-integrated into the modern-day work market, the idea of "having it all" is not as easily attained as advertised. Having a social life, time for relationships, family, children, and household-related duties is difficult enough without the added pressures of a 40-hour work week. Coming in early, staying late, attending work functions, networking off hours, and ensuring commitment to ongoing educational opportunities make combining all the components of work and life feel even more harried. Even when a woman believes she has it all under control, an unexpected event crops up and quickly dissipates that illusion. Any sense of balance swiftly turns to chaos.

Men are in a different position, but they still feel the same pull between work and the other elements of their lives. The difficult balancing act of work and life is often ill negotiated. In general, their relationships are strained, downtime is compromised, availability for loved ones is limited, and the small window of time on weekends is absorbed by chores that were neglected throughout the week. If there is any time left over, it is spent recuperating to do it all again the next week. In this way, not much has changed for the last century's work philosophy.

Both women and men end up on the treacherous hamster wheel of work and life obligations. Often, it feels like there is no escape. When you are on that inescapable, ongoing track, it can feel like there will never be any harmony between the facets of your life and that goals will never be met. How can balance be found, after all, with the influx of conflicting demands we place on ourselves? It can feel like we should always do more.

With only 24 hours available, fitting everything into a day can feel like stuffing all ten fingers in your mouth at once — and then clapping your hands. Even though the feat may be possible for some, that does not mean you need to live up to the standard. Just as some people have bigger mouths and smaller fingers than you, others may have different abilities, needs, or availability that make them better suited to working endless hours on work tasks. Do not beat yourself up if you do not have the stamina, drive, or time to live that lifestyle. Similarly, you cannot blame an employer if you are in a job that requires extraordinary hours and devotion to get ahead. Although long hours, high pay, and a lofty job title may be painted as the ultimate grand slam, your personal success story should be designed by you.

Now is the time to make decisions about the rest of your career life. If you are on a fast-paced track and you do not want to live that way, part of your journey will involve getting on another track. For those who are willing to commit themselves to the requirements of the job track they are currently on but can see other aspects of their lives being neglected, letting certain things go may be the only option. "Letting things go" pertains not only to admitting that you do not have time for certain things in your life, but also that you have to let go of your illusion of perfection.

The idea that a perfect lifestyle exists is problematic from the start. Everyone is different, so the idea that all people should have the same vision of the perfect life is nonsensical. Yet, people buy into the delusion. For parents, sometimes children and work will conflict. The combination of the two will not always function perfectly even when, at times, you feel you have it down to a science. For those who imagine a quick rise to a high salary, the work commitment it takes to get to that point will limit other opportunities in life. You may be able to have it all, but you may not be able to have it all at once.

Establishing your personal vision of a harmonious work-and-life balance may force you to reconsider your current field, setting, and company to ensure compatibility. When you do, make sure you are on the best path for who you are and what you want to accomplish out of your work life. The goals of your nonwork life should be a big priority.

Are You in the Right Field, Setting, and Company?

Perhaps you, like so many other people, have ended up on a life trajectory that was guided more by outside influences than your own true desires or even talents. You may feel that because you have been trained for the field you are in or even invested several years in your current profession, sector, or company, there is no turning back. But just realize, this is your one chance at life. Everything up to this point has been leading to the rest of it. If you are not 100 percent satisfied with the road you see coming up, put on the brakes and take a different path. You and only you are in the driver's seat.

You may have responsibilities that might make it feel as though shifting gears is impossible, but how will you be able to keep up with those duties in the long run if you feel like crashing on a regular basis? Think of the flight attendant speech presented before every takeoff: If the emergency oxygen masks are deployed, put yours on first before tending to others. How well will you be able to tend to other people's needs if you are brain-dead from a dissatisfying work life?

Once upon a time, choosing a college major was a life-altering decision. Today, headhunters claim to rarely seek out a specific major for the professional jobs they need to fill. Instead, the No. 1 thing they look for is simply a college degree. These days, majors are more transferable than a cold at a preschool.

If you want to explore a new path, education can assist you. Before you seek a first or additional advanced degree, consider how college courses will fit into your life. If you choose formal education, you can pave a clean path toward a new career and possibly an increased earning power, but college is not the only form of education at your disposal. One way to explore educational opportunities is to cross-train your talents by checking out other departments of your current workplace. Cross-training your skill set is a move that will benefit you at every level of your rise up even if you discover in the process that the departments you dip into are not for you after all. When you become a high-level contender, having a broad range of skills will set you apart from those who have just been getting by in their jobs.

If you are happy in your chosen field, then congratulations. You are ahead of the game, considering the 85 percent rate of unhappiness at work. What about the sector you have planted yourself? Sometimes, dissatisfaction in a job comes not through the actual duties of the position but rather the niche within the field an individual has chosen. A teacher in a private school may find a public one better suited to her personality. A chef in a bakery might prefer to work in fine dining. A dog groomer may prefer cats. Whatever the case, sometimes a small shift in another direction may be all it takes to quell that itch. You may even be able to move to another department in your current organization if you feel it might be a better fit.

Of course, there is always the possibility that you just may not be in the right organization. This is a tricky situation, because finding the right fit in a company can be a lot like finding the right personal relationship. There are no guarantees that your soul mate company is out there. Just as there are no perfect people, there are no perfect organizations. Although, if you have encountered ongoing frustrations, organizational dysfunctions, head-butting, water-cooler trash-talking, hierarchal hiccups, and the like, you need to sit down and consider whether this is the right relationship for you.

Do not be too quick to assume your dissatisfaction at work has to do with a discontentment in your chosen field, setting, or organization. If it is possible not to jump ship from any of these three elements, you are doing yourself a big favor. Job retention is at a high, according to recent statistics. Do not make the assumption that a switch to another line of work, setting, or company would be easy. With fewer people quitting the jobs they have, the job market may not be as open to accept you even if you do the grunt work you will need to do to make that change. If you feel you must take the leap, be 100 percent sure in your reasoning and take every precaution to cover your backside in the transition.

One more aspect to consider in determining what drives your desire for this promotion is to consider that all you want may simply be to move forward in your organization. You do not need more balance between work and home. You do not hope to work toward some bigger goal. You do not want to make tons of money or earn the prestige of your peers. You are not specifically interested in improving your skill set or learning how to become more productive, efficient, or organized. You simply want to figure out how to get ahead in your specific workplace and see some change. If your goal is simply to learn the exact, fast-paced recipe for how to advance in your particular workplace, you need to figure out specifically what your boss is looking for and values in his or her upwardly moving employees.

Your Boss Holds the Key

While reading this chapter, you may decide that you have no driving desire other than the fact you want to move forward, and earning a promotion is the way to do that. A desire theorist would say there is likely some other motivating factor that is pushing you forward, but for the sake of argument, let us say you simply want to move up in the organization because you do not want to stay in your current position. Most of this book is about taking personal steps toward bettering yourself so you will become a more productive, skilled, and efficient worker. In this section, however, the area of focus is less about you and more about your boss.

Ultimately, earning a promotion is about honing your boss's perception of you and convincing him or her that you are worthy of being brought up in the organization. This reveals the hard truth of office politics: The employee who wins recognition and rewards in the organization is often the one who learns how to read the boss and then manipulate his or her opinions. Consider this brief section the shortcut road toward taking a step up in your career. Remember, though, sometimes if you take a shortcut you miss the best scenery.

To clarify, there is absolutely nothing wrong with carving your path in the organization through catering to the opinions, needs, and values of your boss. Understanding your boss will always benefit you. Neither is there anything wrong with wanting a promotion simply for the sake of wanting some change. The perspective of this book, however, is in attaining a promotion and job satisfaction through personal growth, not just through manipulation of your boss.

According to job expert Marcus Buckingham, the No. 1 way to find job satisfaction is to learn how to use your strengths and feel as though you are accomplishing something at work. Therefore, this book factors in that important aspect of job satisfaction along the entire 90-day process. Determining who you are, what you want, and why you want it are all a part of the introspection needed to earn this promotion and future promotions. With this said, if your goal is more immediate, all you want is a promotion, and you want it now, I have deviated from the course of the natural progression of the book's plan to offer you a clear-cut perspective: Figure out how to please your boss and you figure out an easy way up.

Begin by starting a dialogue with your boss about the philosophy that drives him or her in the workplace. Determine what he or she values, what aspects of productivity in the business are most important to him or her, and what types of priorities he or she works under. In doing this, you will learn what types of traits you should adopt in your own actions to become a promotable employee. Your boss acts according to a self-prescribed value system, so the best way to figure out what type of employee is valuable to your boss you need look no further than right at your boss. He or she is doing everything expected out of the best employees. In addition to figuring out the types of work behaviors your boss values, you should also use this opportunity to learn what you should be doing to show your boss that you are trying to make him or her look good.

When deciding whom to promote, bosses look for employees who best enact the work philosophy to which they subscribe and for employees who make their bosses look good and their job easier. If you want to find a fast track up, it is in your best interest to always know what your boss is doing at work. Pay attention and learn what projects he or she is currently working on, and determine what the related responsibilities of those projects are. With this information, you can create new ways in which to help your boss shine and thus help you to shine. Contributing to your boss's agenda rather than your own may seem counterproductive to your own sense of priorities, but if your goal is to quickly be perceived as a productive, promotable worker, it is important to achieve what your boss deems significant.

Whatever path you take toward earning this and future promotions, goal-setting will be an integral component. Getting what you want takes thoughtful planning and consistent follow-through.

Goal-Setting

In a landmark 1950 Yale study, all members of that year's graduating class were given a two-question questionnaire: Do you have business goals, and have you written down those goals? Only 3 percent of the class had goals they had transcribed. Fast-forward 20 years later, and those 3 percent were wealthier than the rest of the class put together. Many motivational speakers have based their life's theory on this study. This particular study proved to be fabricated, but a college professor recently decided to test this theory herself — with a few minor additions. What she discovered was that the ability to reach goals was most effective when an individual had a clearly written goal with committed instructions toward attaining it and, the new twist, an accountability measure confirmed through weekly communication with a friend.

A person cannot expect to achieve success without a clear definition of what success is and a measure to verify when it has been achieved. High-achieving people often have one characteristic in common. It is not that they all started with money or all have business degrees from an Ivy League school or even a college degree. It is that they planned their path with care. Make that old proverb, "He who fails to plan, plans to fail," your mantra and start thinking about what you want to do with the rest of your life. If you expect life to just happen, you will come to the end of it wondering what happened.

Fruitful goal planning can be likened to the creation of your own garden. Instead of just accepting a grab bag of miscellaneous seeds, be selective of every type you plant. Pick some tomato seed packets. Better yet, get even more specific and set your sights on the Better Boy seed packet. When you decide exactly, specifically, and categorically what you want to plant, take care of those fledgling fruits, nurturing them until you get the perfectly ripe fruit you had planned for.

This may sound tedious, but sit down and plan the rest of your life as you would like to see it flow. Plan your short-term goals: three months (around the time of your promotion), six months, and a year. Plan your long-term goals: five, ten, 20 years, and retirement. Separate your life goals from your work goals, but take both into consideration to provide harmony between the two facets. For instance, if you plan on working overseas within five years, but you want to own a home in that same time, too, you may have a conflict. Thus, you would have to plan to somehow incorporate gaining dual citizenship into your plan to buy land in another country or plan on having a trusty renter who can keep tabs on your home while you are away. Work goals and life goals will sometimes butt heads, but if you plan ahead and organize what you want, you can coax them to blend nicely together. Just be as detailed as possible with exactly what you want, exactly when you want it, and exactly how you will know you have attained it. Without this clear direction of goals, another potential workforce snare may swallow your well-planned intentions, according to Dr. Laurence J. Peter's namesake theory and book, *"The Peter Principle."*

CASE STUDY: GABRIEL VASQUEZ

Gabriel Vasquez, Gunny Sergeant E7

Reserve Liaison United States Marine Corps

I began my military career soon after graduation from high school in an entry-level position. It is 15 years later, and I have advanced from my original entry-level spot through supervisory roles and am now in an upper management position. Currently, I manage groups in training, so now I am responsible for new, entry-level Marines starting out just like I did.

Promotions in the military are attained based on experience and personal goal achievement. To transition from level to level, an individual must put in the time and demonstrate an ability to successfully meet goals relevant to the job title and the needs of the department.

Throughout my career, I have successfully advanced through levels due to a continued attainment of requirements and contribution to mission objectives. I have been able to gain multiple job titles and experiences and have consistently scored above-average marks on evaluation reports.

Setting and achieving goals is an essential component of the Marine Corps hierarchy. To move up levels, an individual must put in the work necessary to meet the requirements. Although I am satisfied with my rate of promotions, I know that if I had set higher goals regarding my level of professional military education and physical training standards,

> **CASE STUDY: GABRIEL VASQUEZ**
>
> I would have been able to compete earlier for upper-level management. This would have given me more leverage on promotion opportunities at the senior advisory level.
>
> I persist in meeting my current level position requirements and plan on continuing to meet those goals during the remaining years of my military career. Additionally, I will build on the goals of the military and those I have set for myself as a Marine by extending this philosophy of goal-setting to my future civilian work life. My current goal is to earn a bachelor's degree before completing my military service.

The Peter Principle

According to Laurence J. Peter and coauthor Raymond Hull, every workforce member is eventually promoted just beyond the utmost degree of her or his potential, and it is there that he or she will not only halt progress as a worker, but also hold back the progress of the organization. When the worker hits the position just higher than his or her potential, that is, that person is promoted to a personal "level of incompetence," the worker will simply flounder about with an inability to keep up. In turn, the organization suffers because it is up to those who have not yet met their level of incompetence to produce the real work that keeps the organization on track.

Although the Peter Principle is based on sound research, the idea behind it might lead you to believe that, when applied to your personal promotion-related quest, you might one day meet an end to your abilities. Knock that idea out of your head. The Peter Principle is mentioned here in the context of your goal setting to provide forewarning to those elements that could possibly hold you back. The theory is used to caution organizations of the principle's potential and, thus, offers solutions to its negative effects. Thus, the theory is positioned from the employer's point of view. That is, organizations are warned against promoting those with incomplete skill sets and should consider lateral employee moves before upward ones. Those organization-focused objectives, although potentially insightful, are minimally helpful to your plight at this point, so let us apply it instead in reference to your goal setting.

If it can be said that workers climb to their level of incompetence, the trick to avoiding this trap, then, must be to maintain an ever-growing level of competency. It is true that some skills and abilities will, by some standard, cap out at some point in line with the intrinsic potential of the individual. We all have different natural talents, after all, so it is not a stretch to suggest that some skills and abilities come easier to others and, to some, may just not be possible. A person who is a mathematical genius, for instance, may simply not naturally have social skills. However, that is not to say that she cannot perform social skills or is unable to train that part of her skill set. Instead of accepting the supposed limits of your competency, then, be prepared to seek new ways to better those things you are good at and those that could potentially hold you back. There is no reason to believe that you must succumb to a wall of incompetence when, ultimately, you are the one in charge of your own growth. Goal setting for ongoing learning is the best defense.

In this chapter of dissecting your work-related goals we have examined why you want what you want, how to plan for these, your personal vision of work and life balance, and how the illusion of incompetence can be just a lesson of ongoing education and good planning. The answer to all the potential hurdles related here is the same. Whether the hurdle is found in the miswants that divert you from true happiness, a failure to nurture the balance between work and life, or the potential level of your own incompetence coming at you head on, the answer can be found in goal setting.

Goal setting is proven to be the best road map for people who want to continuously grow in their lives. Just as you cannot find your way to a town you have not visited without a clear, complete map, you cannot find your way to the goals in your life without strict specifications. You can build up toward any ambition in your life with a detailed plan of well-established goals and directions for how you will get there. To successfully control all the factors that work against you, however, you must be specific in your goal setting, you must take action to meet your goals, and you must stick with them until they reach their maturity and are attained to your satisfaction.

When you have specific goals in place, you will discover something new happening. Because you have taken your future into your own hands, you will find that it is up to you to seek the opportunities to meet your goals.

Possible Pitfalls:

- Be mindful of the miswants that will never satisfy you.

- Maintaining harmony between work and other aspects of your life can be hard work. Make sure you are making the appropriate concessions.

- Consider all aspects of your current job before placing the blame of your dissatisfaction on your field, setting, or organization.

- Do not be fooled by the roadblocks that make you feel incompetent. Take them as a suggestion to keep learning more.

- Be specific in your goal setting and ensure that you keep up with them.

CHAPTER 3

Seeking Opportunities

This week's checklist:

- Read the newspaper or a reliable online news source daily to stay abreast of global, national, and local trends.

- Ask coworkers what they see could be improved in the organization.

- At a meeting, casual discussion with your boss, or through e-mail to your boss, bring up an idea for one way in which you can improve the efficiency of the office. Then, follow through.

- Map out a trend of your workplace. Take it from its current state to how you see it evolving in the next five years.

- Seek out or create an opportunity in your personal life. For example, if you have been meaning to get into better shape, wake up a half-hour early each morning and take a walk.

Sitting in an office, side by side, were two young employees of a medium-sized organization. Andy, the smarter of the two, was always busy performing work tasks to efficient completion. Alex, not only inferior in intellect, but also in looks and charm, was also wheedling away at the tasks at hand but much more slowly and efficiently. Andy and Alex have both been working in the same office for the same amount of time. Their same job titles were based on similar work experience and education. One of them is going to be getting a promotion at the end of this month. So, which one is it going to be, Andy or Alex? Under different circumstances it would more likely be Andy. Production and affability are sure-fire ways to win the race. But in this scenario it is Alex who is the promotion winner because he is the one who took the time to seek out opportunities for growth and recognition.

You have established a specific plan full of goals you will meet at work, but when you start to enact the plan you will find that merely identifying your objectives and working to attain them does not magically open up doors of opportunities. At times you will have to locate those doors, sometimes you will have to create those doors, and every time you will have to be proactive in going through those doors. Following through on your goals will always be contingent on your ability to find or create and then seize opportunities.

CHAPTER 3: SEEKING OPPORTUNITIES

Often, those workers who are dissatisfied with their lack of upward momentum at work get so caught up in their feelings of unimportance they fail to recognize that the people who are moving up in the organization are no better at their jobs, no more qualified, and no more spectacular. The people moving up around them do so simply because they are taking charge of their own destiny and seeking out opportunities for growth. Wallowing in the bad luck of being left behind does nothing for an individual. Time is wasted waiting around as if the boss is going to do all the work of seeking qualified employees.

Your boss wants and needs good employees to move up in the organization. However, he or she is already busy with regular work. Occasionally, a top-notch employee will catch the boss's eye, but it is up to the employees to voice their desires to move up in the organization. Making it known that you are goal-oriented and would be grateful for opportunities to show what more you can do for the organization may be all it takes to get the ball rolling. Tell your boss that you have high aspirations for yourself, that you are a loyal employee and want to move up in the organization, and that you want to keep growing with the company. This way, you have opened up the promotion-related dialogue with your boss and revealed that you are a valuable, dedicated, and upwardly mobile employee.

Letting it be known that you are a contender for new growth opportunities is merely the first step. Your boss is aware of your goals, but it is up to you to fulfill them. Opportunities sprout up everywhere. Although you have voiced your desire to seize growth opportunities, your boss still has other employees to choose from when determining who best fits an opening. Thus, it is up to you to stay abreast of all office happenings so you are positioned to offer yourself up immediately when this type of chance comes up. The supplementary approach is to stay entrenched in the mix of the office so you are poised to create opportunities for yourself. Almost any office happening and discussion can be a catalyst for creating opportunities. Even worldwide happenings, such as technological advances, could be a source of inspiration.

A promotion is not a popularity contest. You do not win the opportunity to rise up solely because you are liked. You win because you signed up for the race, trained hard, and crossed the finish line with the most strength. Much of the strength you will need to win comes from tenaciousness in tending to your own path, so you must always keep your eyes open for your next possible opportunity.

Looking for Opportunities

Become the office snoop. This does not mean you should spy on Betty in cubicle three or dig through your boss's trash. It means you always need to have your ear on the door of opportunity. If someone is switching out of a department or another is quitting all together, you need to register this information and analyze it for applicability to you. If there is talk of a new plant being built in Beijing, you need to contemplate your openness to an overseas move. If moving away is not your desire, consider the likelihood of new positions being created, such as head liaison to Beijing communications, for example. How fast can you pick up Mandarin? Also, other positions could open locally, vacated by people internally who move to the newly created positions.

Often, opportunities will arise and need an immediate fill. The first person perceived as being available may be the one who gets the chance. This means that if your boss does not see you as an available person, you will not even be considered. Being an available employee means being the person who is always ready to work, always on the lookout for chances to shine, and always willing to give a little extra. Sometimes all it takes to be that person is vocalizing that you are that person. Otherwise, your boss may not have reason to know you are actively seeking growth opportunities at work.

Telling your boss that you are available for new opportunities is an important part of the equation, but doing this alone will not secure your place as the front-runner choice. Keeping up on everything that is happening at work and everything that is happening in the world that could affect your workplace is another essential component. By becoming attuned to the factors that could precipitate an opportunity, you will beat your boss to knowing there is a need for people. Anticipate that need before your boss, and you will be poised as the first person considered.

Your boss would much rather have a go-to person in mind than be forced to scan the crowd of workers for an appropriate fit and still not be confident the job will get done. Thus, you need to save your boss the time of locating the right person and the worry of not knowing whether he or she has made the right choice. You do this by letting it be known that you are always open for new opportunities, preemptively offering yourself up for a possible opportunity, and always seeing projects and tasks through to accurate and efficient completion.

The information is out there. You just need to be the one to receive it and be prepared to analyze it for possibilities. You should get to know the people in human resources. You do not need to become their new best friend, but it is good to give them an idea of an actual human being to go along with the paperwork edition of your name. If openings do come up, they are more likely to suggest your name if they know who you are. It is just one simple move that you have control over in the big game of interoffice networking.

Sometimes opportunities will be made necessary by the regular needs of the office. Other times, opportunities will come about through changes, advancements, or growth in the office, technology, business, your specific industry, or some other facet of the world at large. Just about anything could spark a need in your office that will lead to an opportunity for you. You must put yourself in the middle of it all to be ready to seize the opportunity before or, at least, just as the need arrives. However, you should also be putting your feelers out for ideas that will help you create opportunities.

Creating Opportunities

An upward move may not be there when you desire it. This can be from the downward economic trend beginning in 2008, the spike in the number of job-quitters, and a mercurial marketplace for new job opportunities. Even if you are actively looking for potential opportunities, the right one still may not come up. As such, when you ensure you are properly groomed for a promotion opportunity, you may have to create accenting opportunities on your own. For example, if you hear about a new department opening up, you need to be there on the cusp of its conception, dreaming up your perfect, and applicable, niche in that segment of the workplace. If you hear that a higher-level executive is preparing for an upward move, learn more about this person's current job and perch yourself closer to his or her responsibilities if you can. If the market is showing indications of an innovative technology or a shift in market trends, consider how this could affect your organization or lead to a potential advancement for your organization.

In the absence of opportunities to show you are ready for advancement, you need to demonstrate you are valuable. You need to create your own opportunities. There is no better way to show how much you can do for the organization than to create a new way to advance the organization. Anything can be inspiration. Think about what you see is missing from your organization. Think about what other similar businesses are doing that yours is not. Think about ways your organization could make more money, be more productive, and create a better product. Put those ideas together and conceive a plan that will benefit the organization. Be an innovative thinker. If you are able to initiate a good opportunity for the business, your reward could be to head that project.

The mistake many unsatisfied workers make is sitting back and waiting for things to happen. In looking for an opportunity for personal growth, you may be tempted to take the same approach. What may appear to be an absence of opportunities is simply a blank slate for you to fill with your good ideas. The usual interpretation of opportunity is contingent on waiting for what your supervisors hand down to you. These opportunities are not coming through your initiative; instead your supervisors, employers, and bosses are creating them for the employees to seize. Do not wait for the opportunities to be handed to you. Put yourself in your employer's shoes and imagine how he or she could be creating opportunities for the organization and, therefore, for you.

Your employer, and likely your boss too, have a vested interest in ensuring forward movement for the organization. If the organization makes more money, the boss makes more money. So, it is in his or her best interest to keep thinking of new ways to find efficiency and create a better product. In your position, even if you work on commission or own stock in the company, the rewards of oiling the machine are not always immediately obvious. If the company makes more money you may get a bigger holiday bonus, but your reward may be neither guaranteed nor immediate. If the company starts a new system where work gets done faster and with more efficiency, you may feel a slight lessening of your workload but not to the degree that it does much for you.

When considering what you can do to advance your career, try to imagine that you own the company. Take notice of all the ways money and time are wasted. Think up ways to control the bottom line. Create a plan for making the machine run more smoothly, efficiently, and with more productivity. Your reward will not be the same as if you were the company's real owner, but imagine what the potential trickle-down effects could be. Seeking ways to improve the organization will, in turn, contribute to your eventual reception of rewards because you will end up working for a more productive company. But you will also find rewards through being the person who cares about the potential for the organization, for creating ways to improve it, and for showing your employers, supervisors, and bosses that you can make things happen.

Whether you find a good opportunity or create one yourself, you must follow through in all steps of the process to make sure it is a worthwhile experience for the organization and yourself. Being proactive is a part of seeking opportunities, creating opportunities, and following through, but there is more to being proactive than finding and following through on opportunities. Being proactive is about taking responsibility for the path of your life by anticipating the next steps and the means by which to follow through to efficient completion. To be successfully proactive, you must have a working sense of foresight.

Honing Your Foresight

Professional futurists can walk into an office and predict what opportunities will be available to that organization years in advance. You need to have that capability. As Harlan Cleveland, former NATO ambassador, said, "Futurism should be the 'second profession' of everyone."

The school of thought behind developing foresight and the abilities of futurism to help shape the future evolved throughout the 20th century. The earliest versions of professional futurism came in the form of think-tank meetings put together to understand what the trends of impending wars would mean to the future of the country. Now, futurism advocates understanding how much can be learned about the future through thoughtful analysis of today's trends. From that understanding stems the ability to find and create opportunities by which to improve the future of organizations and the world as a whole.

Instead of focusing on events that are occurring today, futurists look for trends to help guide their projective planning. Events happening in the world now tend to be fleeting, but trends have a slow evolution and the ability to be molded for future significance. To locate trends, futurists are always purposefully scanning media and the world around them for indications of evolving ideas. When a futurist finds a trend that holds potential for his or her future, the future of an organization, or the world, he or she analyzes it.

Trend analysis is the process of identifying a trend; assessing its potential; and identifying its causes, effects, and changes. If you can implement trend analysis in your workplace, you will become confident in your ability to grasp future opportunities for your organization and yourself. Although trend analysis, as a professional method, comes in a variety of forms, you can easily add a nontechnical version of it to your repertoire of work tools.

In addition to staying connected to the world's trends through ongoing attention to relevant media, trends are continuously happening at work every day. Look around your workplace. What is happening right now? If you work in the restaurant industry, for example, you will recognize a trend toward wanting more sustainable agricultural practices. To understand the trend and apply it to the future, take its analysis to the next step and imagine specific scenarios or hypothetical projections for the trend's applicability in years to come. In this case, an imagined scenario might include a future in which all restaurants will strive to improve sustainability in their agricultural practices. You can plot out the future of the practices as you envision them evolving, by creating a projection map. For this example, you would chart out the future of sustainable practices with a list of your specific projections. In doing so, you will glean potential opportunities ahead of their time.

You can apply these techniques to any trend in any industry. Paying attention and following your trend observations to a forward-thinking conclusion will help hone your foresight. Having good foresight will make you a valuable employee and will give you an advantage in finding and creating opportunities through which to move ahead in your career. Through your heightened foresight, you will start to recognize the opportunities available to you and will be more prepared and confident to be proactive in following through on them.

Become a Pro at Being Proactive

Characteristics that can limit individuals in relationships and day-to-day living are the same ones that can hold people back in the workplace. Poor self-esteem, pessimism, shyness, sense of entitlement, fear of failure, and a tendency toward laziness are common blocks to upward mobility in all facets of life. You certainly cannot rewrite history, but you can tackle them now, one by one, so they do not hold you back any more than they already have.

What is it that has held you back, either in your personal or professional life, thus far? Are you afraid to appear boastful of your successes, so you refrain from broadcasting them to people who matter? Is it difficult for you to tackle certain tasks for fear of failure? Do you feel undeserving of success, pessimistic toward your future, tired of trying, or feel like everyone is out to get you? These are all roadblocks that you are responsible for tearing down if you want to succeed.

The first thing you need to stop doing is placing outward blame. The blame game is one played by almost everyone at some time, but, even though it is true that others may want to thwart your success, your success can only be thwarted if you let it. Blaming others for your failure is a battle you cannot win. Others will get in your way, either for personal gain or just because they can, but that does not give you license to give up. If you see a speed bump, slow down a little bit, but do not stop the car altogether.

You are seeing new opportunities every day and are coming up with good ideas for the organization that will also benefit your career. Do not let anything hold you back from exploring these opportunities. Instead of being reactive to the opportunities, make a conscious effort to be proactive. Reactive people let things happen in their lives. Proactive people, on the other hand, make things happen in their lives.

Being proactive can be simply described as having the ability to see a potential for choice and being able to conceive of and implement the best course of action. The potential choice may involve a trend you have observed and want to expand on for future improvement, an opportunity that arises without your having initiated it, or a potential opportunity you want to cultivate to your or the organization's best advantage.

When presented with the potential for choice, which is happening at all times, one should tackle the underlying question head on. Instead of resorting to reaction, create and enact the best course of action. The best course of action is the one that will bring you and the organization the most fruitful results.

Example of a Proactive Approach

You read a story in the newspaper about a new accounting program that can streamline bookkeeping procedures. You recall overhearing your boss talk to a coworker about the money that has been wasted in the organization due to inefficiencies in accounting. Here is a potential for choice. A reactive person may register a potential for opportunity, but he or she will ignore the call and simply wait for a change to happen. The reactive person convinces himself or herself not to take action because he or she is not in the accounting department, does not want to risk speaking up about a potential opportunity, and is not willing to take control of a situation when there is no confirmation the work will pay off. A proactive person, on the other hand, will recognize the trend of better technological tools, will seek further information on the new accounting program, will consider the technology's applicability to his or her organization, and will discuss the technology with his or her boss. The proactive person recognizes the constant flow of opportunities and consistently seeks and enacts ways to accept the challenge to seize control of his or her own personal growth.

Being proactive in your career puts you in control. When you vigilantly seek ways to improve yourself at work, you will suddenly be presented with a vast array of potential opportunities. When you grab those opportunities and create plans to use them to your and the organization's best advantage, you will create fruitful outcomes. When you treat every day as a chance to be proactive, you will create a future full of more opportunities and success.

You are in ultimate control of how your life will flow. Do not sit back and let things happen to you. Take control of the potential opportunities and transform them into success.

Although you have taken strides in introspection, future planning, and finding potential for opportunities, before asking for a promotion you must ensure that the perception of your work performance does not hold you back. You could be a nearly perfect employee up to this point, but as a measure of good housekeeping you must ensure that all evidence of your job performance is properly portrayed and maintained.

Possible Pitfalls:

- Do not miss potential opportunities.

- Do not get discouraged if your ideas are not embraced. Keep trying.

- Avoid placing blame on others for your setbacks. If you take control of your destiny, no one else has the power to sidetrack your goals.

- Do not wait for opportunities be given to you. Actively seek out and create them.

CHAPTER 4

Cleaning Up Your Job Performance

This week's checklist:

- Keep a detailed log of everything you do at work this week, including things not work related that may drain your productivity.

- Seek out and engage in at least one nonprofessional and one professional learning opportunity.

- Make a concerted effort each morning this week to start your workday with a positive attitude.

- Every day this week, begin your work promptly on time or early and end your workday no earlier than your expected hours of work dictate.

- Seek out an opportunity to solve at least one problem in the workplace.

Even the hardest-working, most efficient, and productive employee can find something on which he or she can improve. In anyone's life there is always room for improvement. You may be perfectly content with your work efforts thus far, but if you take apart the aspects to your job and yourself as a person and employee, you will always find ways in which you can improve.

If you are already fully aware of the deficiencies in your work performance, this could bode well for you in this process. This may indicate that you are simply an extraordinarily introspective individual. On the flip side, you may have received indication from higher-level employees in your organization that your work has not been entirely good.

Asking for a raise when your current job performance is questionable may be your worst mistake yet. You cannot justify asking for more money, more responsibility, or a better title if you have not satisfactorily maintained what you already have been given. When analyzing what you need to do to ensure a clean record of job performance, often what you will end up managing is merely the perception of that job performance.

Perhaps you think your performance has been up to snuff thus far. Well, so do all the other people who are trying for something better. To ensure you successfully create the perception of a positive job performance record, you will first need to deeply scrutinize what your job performance has been so far. Your boss certainly will.

Take a fresh look at the history of your work performance. Use past reviews for concrete information and accent these accounts with your firsthand, personal understanding of the work you do. Documentations you have maintained will help, but notating brainstormed recollections will work, too.

To be perceived as a quality worker, the burden is on you to showcase your hard work. Doing a good job is only a part of the equation. You need to be cognizant of and prepared to promote every nuance of what it is exactly that you do for the organization. You need to demonstrate you are taking steps to ensure your ongoing dedication to continued education. You need to do all this with a positive attitude while keeping up with the expectations of your workplace, such as contributing an appropriate number of hours and supplying evidence of ongoing productivity. You need to tend to these facets of the job and more, plus find creative ways to showcase all that you do for the organization without appearing boastful.

The first step toward showing your boss that you are a positive contributor is to know exactly what you do. You do your job day in and day out, so you know it best. However, if pressed to describe the duties of their daily job, many workers fall short on a clear explanation of their exact value to the organization. Worse yet, if they take the time to peel apart the layers of their daily work they often find they do far less than they imagined that they do.

Know Exactly What You Do

You perform the tasks of your job day after day, yet if someone were to ask you tomorrow, "Just what is it exactly that you do?" could you answer the person with an in-depth summation? Could you write up a report on what you do day after day, hour after hour and, even, minute to minute? The minutiae of your day may seem trivial if you take it apart piece by piece.

> 9:03   Sat down at desk.
>
> 9:04   Turned on computer
>
> 9:05   Checked MySpace inbox

The bottom line is that you may not be doing as much actual work as you think you are. Maybe you will find that you are doing a good job of working while at work, but you will find areas in which you can improve or specific reasons why you are not getting the recognition you deserve. Maybe you will find that you are doing an excellent job. Whatever you find, recognize this is a fact-finding mission. You are doing this research on yourself so you know what you are going to be selling your boss when you make the jump from planning for a promotion to requesting one. So what if you need to do a little cleanup and ego-healing before you take the leap?

Take a moment now to brainstorm every detail of your job. Write down the main tasks of your work, the grunt work, the problems that come up that you have to tend to, and anything that you have ever done in the name of getting your job done. You may discover you have fewer or more duties than you realized. You may find that many of the details of your job you do not do on a daily basis. You may even realize that you do many things that could be done better, more efficiently, or that could be cut out altogether. The point of this exercise is to become reacquainted with your job so you remember what your job is all about. You will be able to comfortably relay your job's details, as needed, to your boss during this process. You cannot expect to ask for more responsibility if you are unsure you have been successfully maintaining your current responsibilities.

Based on your reintroduction to the tasks of your job and your week's work on identifying those time-drainers that get in the way of completing essential tasks, imagine what a schedule of efficient productivity at work would look like for you. Factor in the most important aspects of your job and tune out the details that waste your time or are not essential to the job. This week, strive to follow this schedule of efficient productivity. By focusing on doing your job efficiently, comfortably, and productively, you will do more work, but you will not feel overwhelmed.

Following a more efficient workday plan will allow you to be more productive. So, you will get more done, but you will feel more relaxed and able to take a more objective look at your work life. One aspect most workers should consider is how up to date they are on the trends of their professions. To keep your working knowledge fresh, you must actively seek ways to continue your education. If your profession has an established set of guidelines for continued education, keep up on it. If your profession has no set standards, establish them yourself. Then, actively seek opportunities to continue your professional education.

Continued Education and Ongoing Learning

Sure, keeping up with trends and innovations in your field is a product of simply doing your job, but an all-encompassing knowledge is gained not just through practice but good old-fashioned educational opportunities.

The Internet is a virtual smorgasbord of prospects. There, you will find professional networking portals by which you can meet others in the field who might have something to teach. Or you can find literature, educational meetings, organizations for your field, and college courses that could accent your knowledge base. Inquiring with your supervisors about out-of-pocket costs is a win-win situation. If the company does offer reimbursement, you can pick up valuable information on its dime. If it does not, they now know you are the type of employee who is willing to put in the time to grow in your profession and put that knowledge to work for them.

Professional networking portals are an excellent way to seek educational opportunities. For example, building an online relationship with a professional peer can provide you valuable insight from a new perspective. This relationship does not need to take a large commitment of any resources for it to be a positive addition to your life. Spending a small amount of time per week in discussion with another person in your field is a good way to learn new things about your profession in the context of an entirely different setting.

Another way to use professional networking portals to your advantage is by joining in with a group. Members of professional networking portals often conglomerate into groups based on profession, organization type, and region. Depending upon what new information you want access to, strike up an online friendship with those in the group who best fit your needs. Or, find an organization to join that will align with your area of work. BNI, Business Network International at **www.bni.com**, is a business referral organization that may help you connect with an individual or company to suit your needs. Additionally, consider finding a volunteer opportunity that will both benefit others as well as aid in your desire to get to know other businesspeople. The Business Professional's Volunteer Network at **http://sociallyresponsible.ning.com** is a helpful resource.

The Internet can also be a good way to find current literature related to your profession or organizational setting. Be leery, of course, of what sources supply the literature. As we have been made aware in recent years, not all Internet sources are reliable. Stick with sites that have a professional affiliation or that have a name you recognize and trust. You should be able to spot those sites with unreliable information, but it is always better to err on the side of over-skepticism than allow yourself to be duped by erroneous literature. Blogs, news sites, and other types of online media can also be valuable sources of new ideas. It should be repeated, though, that nothing on the Internet should be read without recognizing that the information is heavily subject to the biases of those who wrote it. That is not to say you cannot learn from these types of media, simply that part of what you should learn is how to garner wisdom in the midst of subjectivity.

Educational meetings come in many forms. Some, for example, are presented in affiliation with professional organizations. These types are often more costly than a generalized course, but the monies collected are required to pay guest speakers who have found success in your field, cover organization costs, and put together specialized courses with information that can be directly applied to your line of work. Some educational meetings even come with professional training certificates based on the meetings' curricula. Although you should not feel obligated to take courses based on receiving a piece of paper at the end, a training certificate may contribute to future success in your career. Bosses appreciate employees who seek specialized information, new research related to their profession, and new ways to accent professional knowledge. Information seekers are valuable employees. So although professional certification courses can be costly and time consuming, they are a wise investment for the knowledge you can gain and the piece of paper that may remind your boss you are a professional committed to the industry.

Joining up with a professional organization or even a meeting of like-minded business professionals can be a good way to accent your career. You will learn from people in the field and have access to a variety of perspectives. Networking is always a potential aspect, of course, because you never know what valuable connections you can make. If you already feel time pressed, consider that many of these meetings occur regularly or on schedules that can fit into the strict time constraints of working people. The option of online meetings is a good one, as well. As busy as you may feel, there is always time to learn and do something good for yourself. The trick is in doing it in such as way as to avoid the creation of a new source of stress.

On the furthest end of the educational opportunity spectrum is committing your time to earning a college degree. Perhaps you already have one college degree and have thought of going back for another type or higher level. Maybe you did not start or finish one in the first place. Whatever the case, it is never too late to go back to school. Combining the elements of your life now with taking classes may seem daunting, but there are many options that can make it work. Online, weekend, and night courses are a good option. Most important, consider why you want to go back to school. Before jumping in to a potentially stressful, costly, and time-consuming obligation, make sure it is a wise career and life move.

Many professions require a certain number of hours of continued education. If yours is one, make sure you are up to date on those requirements. Make it your goal to keep a tally of formal and informal education you have sought to contribute to your knowledge base. Learning is always a good thing, and your supervisors will admire that devotion to your job and their organization — even if you need to subtly point it out to them.

Your employer will appreciate your attention to keeping up with new knowledge. Tending to ongoing learning indicates that you are an individual who cares about the job and presenting yourself as a positive employee.

Educational opportunities aside, you can take immediate action toward presenting yourself well in your workplace. A simple attitude adjustment can do wonders for your professional appeal.

> ### CASE STUDY: DOROTHY OTTERPOHL
>
> Dorothy Otterpohl (Retired)
> Regional Manager Reservations Services
> Western Region
> Hilton Hotels Corporation
>
>
>
> Although the bulk of my career was spent in the hospitality industry, I did not take any specific steps in the beginning toward grooming myself for this particular line of business. I started my working adult life in the positions that were available to me and then consistently made strides toward achieving higher-level titles.
>
> As a management-level executive, I was responsible for making decisions regarding the future of existing employees in the organization. As well, I was required to assess the potential of possible hires. There are many different means by which to gauge the promise of an individual in terms of how successful he or she might be in a given position. I used many different formal and informal methods. One measure I often used pertained to analyzing the higher education choices of the individual.
>
> This method is not an exact science, but I found it to be a successful way to look at whether an individual might be a good fit for the organization. Accordingly, if an individual had selected a major in college that would require he or she follow through on further education, such as graduate school, but had not done so, it always made me wonder. My concern was about what type of person would invest years as an undergraduate but not press forward to essentially "seal the deal."
>
> Of course, an individual in this position could end up demonstrating high-quality skills and the necessary requirements, but people should understand they will be judged by the perception of their background. They may have to work harder to make up for spotty work histories, incongruent patterns in the educations they have and the future they desire, and other indicators for which they will be judged right or wrong.

Cultivating a Positive Attitude

High-level executives continuously name a positive attitude as the top desirable trait in employees. And it should be. If we all wore our achievements like merit badges on our chests, the playing field might be a more equitable showcase of reward per evidence of productivity. What does show is our ability to demonstrate that we want to be at work providing good service and are ready to produce.

The one sure-fire way to plant that productivity perception is through a positive attitude. Having a positive attitude does not translate to sycophantic tendencies It is not about being phony and "kissing up" to your supervisors. Even if that were the case, you would not come across well if you were only puffing up in the presence of the potential promoters. A positive attitude is not about putting on a show to make yourself look good. It is about cultivating a genuine positive attitude for your benefit.

A negative attitude can be hard work and can wreak havoc on your physical and mental well-being, in addition to simply getting on the nerves of others who have to deal with you. Positive thinking, on the other hand, has been linked with physical health, longevity, and success in one's personal and professional life. Even if your supervisors do not consciously recognize this, new evidence suggests that a positive attitude in the workplace is contagious. According to the 2007 article, "Anticipated Group Interaction: Valence Asymmetries in Attitude Shift," positive workers positively influence other workers, while negativity breeds more negativity.

Some days you wake up and know that you do not feel like going in to work, dealing with people, or even getting out of bed. Everyone has those days, some more frequently than others. Instead of letting the beginnings of a bad mood get you down, make a vow now to appreciate every day for the new opportunity it is. There is a reason you chose the job you are in and styled your life the way it is now. If there are aspects of your life that regularly get you down, know that you are in charge so fix the things you do not like, but do not fall into the trap of a personal pity party. Fix the things you do not like so you can enjoy the things you do like. Work toward continuously adding more things to enjoy. Spending your time in negativity is a waste. There is no reason not to have a positive attitude.

While you are getting ready for work, keep telling yourself how excited you are to start the day. There are so many things to look forward to and be grateful for, so run those exciting things through your head. Walk through the doors of your office with those feelings of excitement for the day ahead of you. Revel in the good things about your life, your job, the people you enjoy, and all that you want to accomplish today and for the rest of your life. Keep pointing out to yourself all that is good in your life and, soon, the things that break your positive attitude will fade away and seem far less important. You do not have to put on a fake smile or simply pretend to be positive to present a positive attitude. Faking positivity is the worst way to go.

Faking positivity does not fool anyone and inhibits your own ability to achieve a genuine positive attitude. You need to believe that your life is positive to feel positive, and then you can present that feeling to the world through your exterior presentation. Negativity is the bad habit that interferes with that potential reality. Instead of allowing the bad habit to take over your mood, replace it with the better habit of always looking on the bright side. Even if you do not believe it at first, your perseverance will eventually win over the part of you that wants to be negative.

In addition to a positive attitude, work expert Donald Asher asserts that top managers acknowledge hard-working productivity as another key quality of promotable employees. Neither hard work nor productivity is as simple to gauge as one would think. An employee may appear to be hardworking when, in reality, he is merely pretending to be hard at work. Productivity should and can be measurable, but it too is often open to tricks of illusion. To earn the perception that you are hardworking and productive, your best bet is to genuinely be hardworking and productive by putting in the appropriate hours and then some, showing your dedication to the job day after day by tending to all the tasks of your job and then finding even more to do, and doing this through an efficient, thoughtful use of your company's time.

Hours, Dedication, and Efficiency

These days, there is no typical workweek. Americans work more hours now than during the reign of the 9-to-5 archetype. From the 1990s to the 2000s, we added a full week to our average year schedule, earning us the top position in the world for number of hours clocked at work. But even in a typical 40-hour workweek, many people cram in a few extra work hours in the nooks and crannies of early morning, late evenings, and weekends.

Modern-day solutions such as flextime, flexplace, compressed workweeks, annualized hours, teleworking, on-site day cares, and myriad technological gadgets provide immediate counterarguments to any suggestion that you cannot fit in the hours expected by your supervisors. When everyone is taking advantage of these innovations to get the job done, you have no excuse for signing onto a job and not adhering to its specific time commitment expectations.

The suggestion here is not that you should work yourself to the bone and let your nonwork life suffer in keeping up with the standard set by your supervisors and the current culture of the workforce. The point is that if you are serious about earning a promotion, you must show a dedication to your job that proves your seriousness. Your dedication will be defined by mirroring and then exceeding the time commitment shown by your immediate peers and higher-level executives.

Just clocking in, of course, is not enough. With those hours you must produce results efficiently. Being at work is about doing your job. Gossiping by the watercooler, perusing non-work related Web sites, taking personal phone calls, and other time-killers are an insult to your employer and a drain on your efficiency. According to a 2008 study conducted by **www.salary.com**, the two biggest work time wasters are personal Internet use and office socializing. A whopping two hours of the average person's eight-hour workday are eaten up by these and other time-wasting activities. The most commonly cited reason for the deviation is that there is not enough work to do, but surely these people's employers would challenge these claims. The bottom line is that if you must surf the Web, come in early to quench that desire, keep the socializing in check, and, if you do not have enough work to do, seek out opportunities. How would you feel about paying someone to play on the computer and chat with his or her friends?

The time you spend on the company's clock should always be used to tend to the company's needs. Keep downtime to a minimum, and keep tending to personal needs to a minimum. You are being paid for your time, so when you are on the company's dime, you should be working. If you find yourself being distracted from doing quality work, have a plan ready to get yourself back on track. For some that may mean taking a quick walk around the office, stepping outside for a breath of fresh air, or playing a quick game of Sudoku. Although your plan may entail doing things that require short bursts of downtime or occasional small windows of time to tend to your personal needs, sometimes a quick pick-me-up is all you need to get back to your job, so consider that attention to yourself as an investment in your ongoing productivity. But keep these pick-me-ups to a minimum, no longer than five minutes, or, better yet, attempt to fit them into scheduled break time slots whenever possible.

In addition to seeking hardworking, productive employees, your boss is also looking for people who can solve problems. Become an excellent problem solver, and become valuable.

Becoming a Problem Solver

Problem solvers are indispensable in every situation in life. What is a good leader if not a good problem solver?

How do you handle a crisis at work? Do you become overwhelmed? Are you able to take charge, or do you pass the challenge on to the known cool head in the office? Become that cool cucumber, the person who is able to step back from the chaos and analyze the situation clearly. Think of it as a math problem with a quantifiable answer. There are many solutions to a workplace dilemma, but being a problem solver is just as much about being able to calmly control the situation and applying a suitable fix as it is about uncovering the right answer. Your supervisors will appreciate your willingness to take charge and begin to see you as the type of leader they want closer to them on the hierarchical stratum.

On any given day, the workplace will become consumed by a new crop of problems. Well-laid plans can go wrong, poorly planned events do go wrong, and unexpected incidents challenge workplace efficiency every single day. To ensure that despite these occurrences things can still get done, the workplace needs a broad selection of problem solvers at the ready to take care of problems efficiently and effectively so all can go back to business. Instead of being just another potential problem, become one of the problem solvers your boss is so desperately seeking.

Never be afraid to offer your solution to a problem. Say your opinion proudly and offer to put your plan into action. Do not stand back and let the problem get solved by someone else just because you are afraid of looking stupid or pushy, or supplying the wrong answer. Everyone can suggest something that could work, so you might as well do some good for yourself and the company and come up with a solution that will work. When a problem arises, stand back and examine what caused the problem, what is happening due to the problem, and what the potential solutions may be for that particular problem. Based on your assessment and a cost analysis comparison of your potential solutions, prepare to broadcast your answer. Because everyone has a different perspective, your solution is likely to be unique. Because you took the time to think considerately about the problem, your solution is likely to be a good one. And because you know the key to problem solving is tackling a problem with a calm, clear head, you can easily score a victory for being an adept problem solver.

Picking up and broadcasting the traits your boss is seeking in a promotable employee is only part of the equation of an effective job performance cleanup. As well, you will want to prepare to hand your job cleanly down to the next person to fill your position.

Preparing to Pass the Torch

Because you now know exactly what you do at work, you can begin some preparations to pass the torch of your current job. Of course it will not be up to you who will be taking over your role, but it is good housekeeping to ensure someone is immediately available to prevent a delay in transitioning. Often, contemplations on promotions are a simple cost-and-reward consideration. If the resources for funding your promotion are greater than the reward to the company (for example, headhunting or internal training costs for your old position), your employer will be less likely to move forward with your promotion.

The goal is not to devote hours of your energy to bringing up an underling to your level in the organization. You simply want to seek out the best candidate to take over your current job and, if appropriate, invite him or her to work with you on a project or simply open up a dialogue about work-related issues. If the opportunity arises during the promotion discussion process, you will be at an advantage if you have managed to solve the problem of finding and grooming your replacement.

In preparing to pass the torch, you will want to ensure the evidence of what you did in your position is in tip-top order. Paperwork and computer documents are a big part of that picture, so next it is time to work toward getting all those other loose ends organized so you can be fully prepared to pass the torch and take the next step forward.

Possible Pitfalls:

- Do not miss out on an opportunity for growth. Pay attention to every aspect of your job to fully assess areas for improvement.

- Move from feelings of entitlement and appreciate that your employer is paying you for every minute of your time. If you waste your time, you are wasting money.

- Keep an eye open to the unconscious ways in which you diminish your level of efficiency.

- Do not make the mistake of assuming your education is over because you have moved on to the real world of work. Ongoing education is an expectation in nearly every industry.

- Do not miss opportunities to practice your problem-solving skills.

CHAPTER 5

Get Organized

This week's checklist:

- Create an office setting that works perfectly with your needs and organizational style.

- Try out a variety of organizational methods for your workspace, paperwork, and computer-based data.

- Create a calendar system that will work for your lifestyle.

- Create a brag sheet to document your successes and project completions.

- Incorporate at least one stress-busting or prevention technique into your work week.

When the idea of organization comes up, people think of putting tangible things in order. However, often what makes us feel disorganized are not the touchable things in our spaces but rather the conceptual aspects to our lives. Feeling disorganized has to do with our inability to manage our schedules, stress, tasks, and dealing with physical clutter. We all have plenty of stuff, both tangible and otherwise, that bogs down our ability to get organized.

Organization can be elusive. Just when you think you have control over your surroundings, something happens that breaks the flow of the seeming calm you had worked so hard to attain. A catastrophe interferes with the rhythm you had found at work, and you instantly find yourself clamoring for control once again. Sometimes you may even backtrack because you become paralyzed by the workload you have to make up.

Work paralysis can strike anywhere. When a home becomes overwhelmed by the items on to-do lists, just sitting there seems optimal over tackling everything on an ever-growing list. Then, nothing gets done. There is so much to do that any semblance of a starting point becomes buried. The workplace suffers the same affliction when feelings of disorganization and uncontrollable to-do lists attack one's ability to feel productive.

In this sense, a to-do list is not necessarily a catalog of all those tasks that need tending to but rather an idea of all that one needs to accomplish on a regular day to feel organized and content. Standard items roll over from day to day. Things such as exercise, eating healthy, spending time with loved ones, cleaning, relaxation, learning, personal care, and the basic duties of one's job are the first level of what people attempt to accomplish to feel sufficiently productive. Yet, when the other pressures of work and life get factored in, these basic items can become neglected or pushed to the side to tackle the pressing items that become inserted in their place. So instead of ensuring that basic items have priority, the mind becomes muddled with a new assortment of to-do items that may not have equitable value.

When you have 100 things you want to get done at work, the tendency is to look at the whole group of to-dos and become engulfed by the big picture. A predisposition toward perfectionism can make tackling to-dos even more intimidating because, with every item on the list, the goal becomes more about getting things done perfectly as opposed to getting things done sufficiently. Instead of expecting that you can do everything perfectly, strive to simply get the things done that need to get done. This does not mean you should accept shoddy work. This means you need to figure out what needs to get done and redefine what that means.

If you can limit your to-do list to those tasks that are essential or that will effect a tangibly positive result, you can cut out some unnecessary work for yourself. The need to feel productive can be convincing in getting us to do a bunch of things that are neither important nor, upon completion, make us feel any more satisfied. Do yourself a favor and start feeling more organized now by eliminating the nonsense that is not that important. For you, that may mean keeping "thank-you cards" on your list but getting rid of "paint fence." In today's world, time is often our most valuable resource. If you are spending it on things that you think need to get done but are interfering with your sense of organization, reconsider the value you are giving to these tasks. You may find that you have been wasting much time on things that do not matter.

The truth is that you can never have complete control over your surroundings. So, instead of striving for organized perfection or complete control, take care of your life's basic needs and then seek out systems to simplify the rest of your life. Weed out the superfluous junk that does not matter and work toward a comfortable maintenance of what you must manage. The first step is to figure out what your basic needs are.

Defining Your Basic Needs

Consider the things you need to accomplish in one day. If you are like most people, you have a standard series of tasks attached to each role in your life. Often, people set themselves up for failure by continuously adding in task after task atop the basic list of things they need to do even before they have successfully managed the basic list. For example, a basic needs list includes those tasks associated with tending to one's home, the relationships inside and outside the home, commitments to clubs, pastimes, organizations, work responsibilities, and basic health requirements.

But when you cannot manage your basic list successfully, you feel disorganized and overwhelmed. When you add more to your basic list before you have mastered what is already there, you feel more disorganized and overwhelmed. Worse yet, many people forget that the additional items added in to their list do not have the same importance or value as the basic needs attached to the core roles in their lives. Then, they end up not doing anything for their basic needs and, also, beat themselves up even more for not being able to manage the added items on their list. Nothing is getting tended to, and they feel just as bad for not giving cousin Frida a call as they do for not taking care of their precious health.

Instead of looking at your list of to-dos as one big, ever-growing list, begin by listing your basic needs away from the other stuff that gets added in. Establish a manageable set of the basic needs you must tend to during the course of a typical day and assume that meeting those needs is all you need to do for the day to be a considered a success. For example, decide that if on any given day you exercised for 30 minutes, ate five fruit and vegetable servings, spent time with your three principle loved ones, learned one new thing at work, and completed the three core duties of your job, you have had a victorious day. Consider this your list of basic needs, and accept that these are your priorities for the basics of everyday organization.

After you have your basic everyday organization under control, do not pierce the harmony you have created for yourself by throwing in everything else all at once. Consider time as your most valuable resource and a commodity that can be made into either friend or foe. Manage your time wisely, and you will see there are enough hours in the day.

Time Management

In a world where being busy is rewarded over being productive, the whirlwind of stress can suck you down faster than you can say "procrastination." Good time management is about being able to efficiently master your available time. It is not about trying to cram in as much busywork as you can. The trick is to use your time wisely to actively produce results.

Studies indicate that only 20 percent time spent working spawns productive results. This means most of our time at work is swallowed by busywork, inefficiency, and time-wasting. Productivity is the major reason we are paid for our position in the workplace, so if we are not creating the results for which we are getting paid, then our time is being ill-spent: Our employers are wasting their money on us, and we are wasting our valuable time. Our time is not being properly managed.

One major contributor to poor time management is the popular tendency toward procrastination. Many people procrastinate. It occurs when people are presented with tasks they feel they cannot do, cannot do well enough, or are less preferable to the other tasks they would rather do. Procrastination becomes a problem when it causes the individual to avoid certain tasks altogether, perform poorly, and create stressful situations based on mismanaged time.

Some procrastinators defend these practices and suggest it is under these circumstances they work best, but this is rarely the case. Procrastination is linked to poor organization and, if not caused by it, can certainly result in it. When certain tasks are prolonged to completion, the procrastinator has difficulty keeping up with those tasks as well as other tasks that get lost in the ensuing disorganized shuffle.

Recognizing the problem of procrastination is the first step toward thwarting it. If you have the tendency to put off until tomorrow what should be done this minute, seize that moment to better understand why you procrastinate. Break that habit as it occurs, and instead of putting off the tasks you normally would, complete them well and in a timely fashion. To do this and to manage the rest of your time more efficiently, the key is in devising an all-inclusive schedule.

Plan your week in advance, factoring in personal time, work time, spare time for contingencies, and basic needs and to-dos. Your basic needs should be a priority and, from there, incorporate your remaining agenda items. You should have a good idea of how much time it takes you to complete certain tasks and how much time you should allot for unexpected contingencies. However, creating a streamlined schedule may take some time if it is to become an efficient template for your ongoing planning.

When you have a good plan for time management, focus on getting things done more efficiently instead of worrying about perfectionism or procrastination, and you will stop kicking yourself when you imagine you are not getting enough done. You want to continue moving forward at work, so now is the time to begin adding more back in your life. Start fresh in the workplace with the establishment of manageable systems to help you get more done.

Establishing Systems

In the 1980s, there was a bumper sticker that stated, "A clean room is the sign of a disturbed mind." Today, like-minded theorists have claimed a similar mantra: Excessive organization is unnecessary. Some experts even claim advantages to disorder, and a few proselytize just what the bumper sticker suggested: Too much organization is a sickness. For the rest of us who are able to keep from organizing to excess and are not obsessive enough to separate every last item in our office by size, shape, color, or function, we can view organization as the sanity-saving tool it can be.

Being organized is not about kicking someone out of your office when he or she does not use a coaster or moves your pencil cup two millimeters to the left. It is about establishing systems that work for you.

Before embarking on the mission of office organization, consider what you have tried in the past that has and has not worked for you. Take into account your particular quirks, like whether you work best with alphabetizing, color-coding, or visual cues. Close your eyes and imagine what usable organization looks like to you. The images that pop into your head may be your best clue into how your inner organizer will best flourish. "Neat and tidy" does not work for everyone. Plenty of people organize best through personal systems that are perceived as a mess by others but for them makes complete sense. Remember, whatever works best for you is your best system of organization.

Because organization system variations are endless, the easiest place to start exploring is by trying out a few specific expert suggestions. Studies show that endless paperwork, clutter, e-mail inbox crowding, and time management are the top stress inducers that can be managed through better organization. Here are simple solutions for these target areas.

Use these suggestions for inspiration, and then create systems that are meaningful to you:

- Use a tickler file for time-sensitive papers, memos, and even self-notes. This is an accordion-style file complete with spots for up to 31 days of the current month and 12 for each month of the year. Consult it at the start of every day.

- Although sticky notes may seem to add clutter to your workspace, the addition of manageable objects is not clutter and may ultimately reduce the unmanageable clutter that can take over your workspace. Color-coded notes that identify tasks related to specific facets of a job can work wonders for many visual thinkers who have a hard time with a computer-based taskmaster system.

- When pressed with a request to add one more thing to your plate, whether it be baking cookies for your child's classroom party or helping a coworker meet a deadline, take a minute before agreeing to anything. Think about your own needs when considering whether you can afford to add something to your agenda or, as in some cases, afford to say no.

Although taking on too much can be destructive, fully consider repercussions of saying no to work opportunities before passing. If you do agree, always consider if a shortcut is applicable. It is all right to buy the cookies occasionally (or even every time). Your time is your own. It is a resource that should be shared only as determined by you, not because you feel guilty or are afraid to say no.

- Conduct an e-mail inbox cleanup no more than four times a day (for example, first thing, mid-morning, after lunch, and at the end of the day). First, weed out the junk. Next, respond to and then file or delete the simple response items. Then, move task-related e-mails into specific to-do folders (for example, personal, work, and financial) and make notations in your calendar for any time-sensitive items. Allow one more daily, scheduled in-box check with a time-constrained designation in which you respond to and take action concerning your to-do folders.

- Establish a schedule for your typical day's activities. Do not expect to follow it exactly on any given day — meetings, time-sensitive tasks, and emergencies will cause regular deviations — but it will help you order what to do on those days when you simply cannot focus.

- Instead of spending ten minutes by the water cooler during break time, invite a friend into your office and do some mindless filing while you chat.

Spend some time playing with these and other organization systems. Practice using them, make changes as needed, and mold them until they work for you. The point of developing a personal system of organization is to make your life easier and to streamline your day-to-day tasks. When you lose control of these elements of your life, it can feel as if your life is out of control. Take care of your basic needs, and then maintain the influx of additional to-dos and you will avoid that out-of-control feeling.

When you get in the groove of using systems to your advantage, you will not know how you ever managed without them. Think of how good it will feel when your boss requests something no one else can find and you whip it out in minutes. Additionally, having a handle on your daily tasks will allow you to get even more organized with the next phase, discovering the maximum way to structure your workspace.

Structuring Your Workspace

At the end of an interview with Albert Einstein, a journalist requested a phone number for any follow-up questions. Einstein pulled out a phone book to look up his number. Perplexed, the reporter asked why he did not have his own phone number memorized. Einstein responded there was no need for him to memorize something when he knew just where to find it. This speaks volumes to the simple truth of organization: Store only what you must.

Although there are many different ways to organize your physical workspace, these three basic rules can work for almost anyone:

- First, like Einstein's brain, you do not want to overload your workspace with superfluous items. Of course you will have some items you will not need access to on a regular basis, but you may need to reference them in the future. Keep only your regularly used items close. Everything else should be placed in a systemized storage file or boxed away from your immediate area.

- Second, experts suggest using an in- and out-box system to tame the paper parade that haunts so many. It will be up to you how you systemize the box system, emphasizing the various dimensions of what comes in and out of your office (for example, bills and memos), to your advantage.

- Third, everything that lives in your office should have its own home. Everyday supplies such as staples, tape, and pens will be roommates in one dwelling, but everything else, even visitors such as office-roaming birthday cards waiting for your signature, need to have a comfortable spot to rest.

If possible, your workspace should appear neat and tidy. Most people see an abundance of objects as clutter. Therefore, you come off as being disorganized. Of course this may not be the case. Some of the most organized and put-together people simply work best with systems that appear disorganized but work for those individuals. If you are one of these people, do not fret. Instead of making yourself unhappy and more disorganized following a system that looks nice but is not user-friendly, stick with the systems that work for you and continuously demonstrate that they do work for you by being on task.

Space organization is similar to the aforementioned daily task systems in that the best method is relevant only to you. This is the space you have to work with, so your best bet is to design it to your specific needs, habits, and tendencies. A coworker may set up her office with three rows of perfectly labeled filing cabinets, but if you do not work best under that sort of organization system, then her well-designed office has nothing to do with you. The goal of workspace organization is to have access to the information and tools you need and to achieve successful maintenance of the tangible details to your life.

Play with the three basic rules to determine how workspace organization can work best for you. After you have a setup you can work under, start planning for the next phase of organization: creating a manageable and beneficial paper trail of your job.

Preparing Synopses of Projects, Duties, and Achievements

This next tactic flows along in the realm of Einstein's ability to organize his retention of only the "need-to-know" data. Instead of bogging down your brain with minute details of your past work, extract the highlights into a synopsis, no longer than one page in length, after you have put it to rest. It is important that you keep track of the projects you complete. This is especially true of the jobs you will want to reference later in promotion discussions, but you do not need to waste space in your brain with all the details.

Creating a paper trail of your work history will also be helpful as you prepare to pass the torch on to your replacement. The next person to fill your position will appreciate the easily accessible guide to what you have been doing, where he or she should pick up from, and what sort of work he or she should expect to be doing in the role. You want the potential for your transition up perceived to be as seamless as possible, and maintaining a log of this sort will ensure this perception. Remember, because promotions are often weighed according to costs and benefits, whatever you can do to lower the costs of your transition will weigh heavily in your favor. Eliminate an aspect of the costs, in this case the costs of training your replacement on what your present position entails, and you have added one more point to your benefit column.

Maintaining a log of your projects, duties, accomplishments, and other memorable aspects of your job is quite simple. When you finish a project, type the details into a prescribed document some like to call a "brag sheet" so you have a traceable documentation of your work. In addition to being a good way to ensure your good work is preserved, you will also find it a helpful reference resource when, for example, a similar project arises or related questions come up from others or you need to update your résumé. It is an easy thing to do and the rewards are huge, so make the time to do it.

After you have tended to your basic needs, thoughtfully added back in the to-dos that you can now manage more successfully, factored in better time management, implemented systems of organization, and have begun your ongoing brag sheet, you will feel calm and confident. Do not let the chaos of life's surprises take over. Do something now to prevent the onslaught of stress from sabotaging the work you have done to attain better organization: Actively prevent stress from creeping in.

Stress-Busting

Lack of organization leads to clutter — clutter in your office, clutter in your mind, clutter in your life — and clutter leads to stress. When you streamline your to-dos, your workspace, your thinking, and your schedule, your stress level will show immediate signs of improvement. But stress will slowly try to work its way back in. Therefore, it is time to allow a few more things into your life: stress busters.

You may hear some complain, "I worked 80 hours this week. I have not seen my husband for three weeks! Who has time to exercise?" Ignore this silly, unspoken competition. It is not a demonstration of skills and effectiveness on the job. It is a meaningless one-upmanship battle where the winner is the fool who has the ability to neglect everything else in the name of being "super busy." It is not admirable, healthy, or necessary in most fields. Sure, in some fields and organizations, you may be expected to defer all else in the name of the job. To get ahead, you may have to adopt that culture and play by those rules. If this is the case in your workplace, you may have a decision to make. In most positions, however, you should have time for work and time for a life. An organizational mentality that discourages harmony between work life and other pursuits is unlikely to have a sense of harmony itself.

Instead of being the victor of the Stress Olympics, go the opposite direction and take care of yourself. Add in a few self-nurturing measures here and there to prevent future stress breakouts. Take your meal in the office and spend your lunch hours taking a walk instead. Purchase or bring in something for your office that creates a sense of calm just for you. For some that might be a beautifully framed photograph of the sea, an aromatherapy candle, a tea percolator for regular tea times, or a weekly batch of fresh flowers. It may sound self-indulgent, but a sliver of calm in your workplace could be the difference between a meltdown and a go-to option for stress reduction. Life can be hard work even on those weeks where you feel as if you have not tried your best. Do not wait for a reason to reward yourself. Nurture yourself regularly as a simple act of maintenance.

Simple acts of self-preservation can go a long way toward maintaining a comfortable daily existence. If you do not take the time to take care of yourself, the peaceful organization you have created will be for nothing. It is your responsibility to take care of yourself.

After you have a better glimpse of who you are in the workplace and what parts of you have been hidden beneath the clutter of disorganization, it is time to begin marketing yourself. You are a brand all your own.

Possible Pitfalls:

- Avoid adopting an organizational system that does not fit your needs or that is not in line with the way you are most productive.

- When structuring your workspace, ensure you keep the items nearby that you use most frequently.

- Do not spend too much time agonizing over the details of your brag sheet. Include only the most pertinent details.

- Remember to take time for yourself. If you do not tend to your own needs, you will lose the ability to tend to outside needs.

- Skip the Stress Olympics and instead work toward maintaining a manageable life style.

CHAPTER 6

Brand yourself

This week's checklist:

- Think of at least three facets that have somehow contributed to your uniqueness and work toward embracing them.

- Ask a friend or trusted coworker to name what he or she sees as your greatest strengths.

- Come up with two positive personal traits you will incorporate into your personal branding.

- Observe a person you admire in your workplace. Determine what his or her two branded traits are and consider how he or she uses those traits positively.

- Incorporate a personal trademark into the everyday presentation of your appearance.

In commerce, it is often not the product itself that gets our attention but the way it is packaged. Although a certain brand of cookies may be the tastiest treat at the store, the name itself could deter the average grocer from trying them. You might be the most productive in your department, have the highest IQ in the entire organization, and the work ethic of ten Abraham Lincolns. However, if you are not showcasing your attributes and accomplishments in the best light, you might as well be hiding in a cubicle behind the dumpster.

Competition is fierce these days, and it is not enough to have the skills and traits that will make you stand out. You have to have a good package and the knowledge of how to promote it. Consider your personal brand. To ensure your marketability, you must have the ability to showcase your best traits and strengths. Part of this process comes through in your daily dealings: In using your strengths to their best advantage you consistently show the world your greatness. But the other part of the process must be purposefully enacted. To cultivate your brand, you must actively hone your best traits and then actively present them across all aspects of your work life.

Just like well-known and loved brands in the marketplace, creating the most advantageous presentation of you must be an operation of deep heuristic design. Rarely is a product branded through dumb luck. Millions of dollars are spent in identifying the most marketable aspects of the products and the brand itself. You may not have the big bucks to research your personal brand, but you do know yourself like no other. Thoroughly search yourself to determine what you as a marketable product look like.

It has been said that all business is about products. Sometimes those products are tangible items such as food, clothes, or electronics. Sometimes those products are services. In all cases, though, the branding of the product is what ultimately sells it. Translated to your success at work, this means you, the brand, should have the skills needed. However, even more important, you should have the means to promote those skills.

The brand of you is a product unlike any other. You have the power to cultivate the perceptions of others by promoting your most memorable and positive attributes. This week you will investigate how you can best cultivate and market your brand. First, you must determine what your brand is.

What Makes You "You"

Stuart Smalley, the Al Franken character in 1980s *Saturday Night Live* skits, provides a good example of the type of self-forgiving introspection you should practice on yourself. Stuart gave himself a proverbial pat on the back every time he passed a mirror. He told himself regularly that he was good enough. He assured himself that, gosh-darn-it, people liked him. In actuality, he was a bit of a weasel, kind of unattractive, and seemed a bit stunted by his innate lack of confidence. Still, he was unique, one-of-a-kind, completely optimistic, and determined to accept himself just as he was. There was no other Stuart Smalley and never will be. I doubt you are anywhere near as nerdy as dear Stuart. However, if you are here seeking help, chances are you are a big enough person to accept that you have flaws that could be holding you back.

Although the word "flaws" has a negative connotation, try to reconsider what it means in this context. Everyone has flaws. Nobody is perfect and should ever expect to be perfect. It is often our imperfections that create our uniqueness. Your flaw may be a crooked nose, a tendency to over-apologize, or an inclination toward dramatics. There is no need to sugarcoat them with a more politically correct name, by calling them "differences" or referring to yourself as being "special." Embrace the flaws you have because they will always be a part of you, even if you eventually erase them. Besides, if you do not acknowledge your flaws, you will never know what you can work on.

Flaws and all, there is only one you. So set those insecurities aside and start focusing on what makes you who you are. Look toward promoting your strengths as opposed to lingering over the what-ifs of how you could be better. You, the brand, are what you have to sell at work, so find the brand that represents and markets you the best. You do not need to be perfect to be appealing to others in the workplace or anywhere else. You just need to be the best version who you can be.

You need to discover what makes you unique and what people appreciate about you. Is it your sense of humor? Is it your ability to think on your feet? Is it your kind heart? Your ability to look put together? Your ability to recall the most trivial information?

Your specific talents may be mere expressions of what makes you unique. Explore your unique characteristics and talents and find how they set you apart. Learn how they can be applied at work. For instance, if you keep the crowd laughing, it may be your ease at client communications that could come in handy in the eyes of your bosses. If you always look pulled together, your attention to detail could be your draw. Even if your best talents seem completely irrelevant to the workplace, they can be worked to your advantage. Enthusiasm in athletics, for instance, can demonstrate tenacity, health, and willingness to try new things. Do not discount anything. Look at everything that makes up the person you are to determine what marketable attributes should make up your personal brand. Part of this process involves considering how you have been perceived thus far by the rest of your world.

Outside Opinions on You

Your mom was wrong; you are not likeable to everyone. No one is. Just as you do not mesh with every person with whom you come into contact, there will be certain people who are not into you. But instead of sulking over the occasional dose of bad vibes thrown your way, look at yourself from the perspective of a person who is not drawn to you, seems repelled by you, or downright detests you. Even if this person's disdain appears unjustified, you can still learn much about yourself and your interactions with other people.

Try to determine what this person does not like about you. If you are lucky, you will find he or she is simply jealous of you, and you may have your answer to what is special about you. Although assuming that the rest of the world is jealous of you would provide a simple solution and one that would instantly serve your ego, do not put all your faith in this rationale. More likely, you simply possess a trait this person finds unappealing. Certainly you could understand, on occasion, you encounter individuals who irk you through the simplest actions. That barista at the coffee shop who insists on rewording your drink request into the appropriate coffee shop-ordered lingo or the receptionist in your office who is always inexplicably chipper and greets you each day with the same pasted-on grin. Occasionally you meet someone whom you simply do not like, with no real explanation. Sometimes people are just not agreeable.

Instead of putting your attention toward trying to get this person or these people to like you, learn from the experience. Try to understand what might rub people the wrong way about you and consider working on it. Do not spend too much time on your possible flaws, though, because your brand is about what you have going for you, not what could detract. Besides, a person may not have any real good reason for disliking you. For example, this person may tend not to like certain characteristics in people and absentmindedly vetoes everyone who possess those characteristics. Whatever the reason for the dislike, you can always learn from the experience. If you figure out what he or she does not like about you, consider whether it is something worth working on. Or, if you discover the reason for disliking you is petty and unfair, you can practice your people skills by testing how well you can navigate a professional relationship with these sorts of people despite recognizing their disdain for you. Finding that someone dislikes you can be hurtful or simply make you angry for the seeming injustice. However, inside the nuisance of those feelings is a potential lesson. Ignore the drama, and seize the learning experience.

Also take into account those people who like you. For example, ask some of your non-yes-man friends what they like best about you. If you are comfortable with it, also try picking the brains of a few coworkers whose opinions you trust. They will have a good idea of your workplace reputation. Make it easy on them and ask what makes you stand out in a good way among your peers. Any answer is good.

Take the information you get from your friends, peers, and coworkers and decipher what it could mean to your brand. "You are always on time" can indicate your devotion to the job. "You always have a smile" may translate to a positive attitude. "You bake the best cookies" could mean someone is trying to get you to bring in a Friday treat, but it could also speak to your thoughtfulness, ability to follow directions well, or any number of things that along with your attuned self-reflection can help you determine your uniqueness in the organization.

Even if you do not agree these aspects are special about you, thoughtfully and appreciatively consider their opinions. After all, you are attempting to determine what perceptions people have about you. These opinions are based on something you are exuding and, ultimately, are the sum of your brand. For example, you may have always believed your willingness to help other people with their life issues demonstrates your kindness. In this way, when considering your brand you may have thought to emphasize this aspect of yourself. However, if the outside perception on these tendencies points to your keen problem-solving abilities, you may want to consider if this perceived characteristic is more true to your talents. It can also be a more promotable trait of your personal brand.

Your brand, although rooted in your genuine uniqueness, is all about presenting yourself in the best light and encouraging positive perceptions in others. Personal branding takes introspection and a concerted effort to present to the world those traits you think are most noteworthy.

How to Cultivate and Promote Your Best Two Brand-able Traits

Brand specialists suggest that, when working toward cultivating and promoting your own brand, focus on no more than two of your most brand-worthy traits. This method works for mainstream products and it works for personal brands. For example, branding strategist Catherine Kaputa suggests finding what she calls your one "big idea." This is what makes you stand out in the crowd. The "big idea" about you, for example, may be your outstanding ability to relate to a variety of different types of people.

Based on your self-reflection and the feedback you have received from others, you should be able to start putting together a big picture of the "you" as perceived in your workplace. From that big picture, pluck your two best and most identifiable qualities. For the sake of example, perhaps you have ethereal warmth and a droll wit. Discover how you can optimize these traits for consistency, appeal, memorability, and applicability to your workplace.

Consistency is important when cultivating and promoting the brand of you. People go to a specific coffee chain because the products are consistent. If you went in to pick up your usual half-caffeinated latte and the barista insisted the store was all out, you would be thrown for a loop. If you are known as being the go-to gal or guy for a pair of open arms and a chuckle, deviations from that standard can confuse those who have bought into your brand. The point is not that you should put up a charade to be what people expect of you; the point is to cultivate only what is true to your nature and share those qualities with all, not just with the people who supposedly "matter."

Be careful in what qualities you choose to promote in your brand for their true appeal. Certain types of humor, for instance, are not appealing to all. Sarcasm, as playful as it may feel to some people, is a pet peeve of many others. Something as seemingly inviting as warmth, which should be a good thing, can have a negative perception. In some cultures or to certain personalities, showings of instant familiarity, even if that is simply your warm personality, might be off-putting, feel fake, or even be frightening. If the consensus from others is that these traits you are choosing to promote are appealing, you are likely on track. But be especially wary, in these first stages of cultivating your personal brand, of how your personality and brand are being perceived by others.

One of the vital points in cultivating and promoting your personal brand is hitting that button of being memorable. You simply being you is a constant reenactment of your personal brand. You being funny, for example, may just be who you are. Enjoy that, savor it, and share it with others. You do not want to go overboard and thrust it in everyone's faces at meetings. This is not how you want to be remembered. But if an idea strikes your funny bone and you want to appropriately share a joke with others, by all means express yourself. Along with simply being your authentic self, find ways to impress others in an appropriate, likeable way. Adorn yourself with signature accessories. Flash your genuine smile to both upper and lower personnel. Buck trends and explore things that feel genuine to you and your personal brand. If you want your brand to stand out, you have to be honest about who you are while still showcasing your uniqueness.

The final important point to cultivating and promoting an effective personal brand in your workplace is ensuring its applicability. You want to be remembered for the happy-go-lucky man or woman you are, so you fit in a polka dot every chance you get: a polka-dot tie, the occasional dotted sock, or a subtle polka-dot print on your business cards. Sure, that may be you, but how does it go over in your workplace? Or, what about your loud-mouthed guffaw that tears down walls of the funeral home in which you work? You should not have to push the genuine you down just to succeed at work, but you do have to consider what is applicable and acceptable in your line of work and the organization you have chosen.

Also, do not neglect the other major point in your brand: physical appearance. After all, appearances do matter.

Appearances

It may not seem fair, but appearances do matter when it comes to procuring positive perceptions. This does not mean you must be drop-dead gorgeous to be deemed attractive. Some of the most attractive people are, by symmetric standards of beauty, not the best-looking.

Attractiveness can be attained through multiple avenues unrelated to one's set of physical attributes. For example, a good personality, a kind heart, and even a dazzling smile can make even the most asymmetric face appear lovely. Anyone can be attractive if they let positive traits shine through.

Appearances, though, are a different story. First impressions are made within seconds of a first meeting but can linger through the rest of the relationship. Rumpled clothes, unkempt hair, and any sort of apathy toward how you present yourself to the world will convey a negative message to the people who work with you. While you are in this process of cultivating your brand, put some consideration into your package. It may go against everything you wish the world was about, but the fact is that people do judge a book by its cover. Make yours presentable.

Your appearance is in your ultimate control. Put some time and thought into your personal hygiene, grooming, and the clothes you put on each day. You do not have to spend an excessive amount of time or money to present yourself well. A good shower and cleansing in the morning is essential. So, too, is heading into work with a tidy hairstyle and well-groomed presentation. Attention to these personal hygiene and habits will ensure you look put together. This is the perception you want associated with your brand.

One of the simplest ways to control other people's perceptions of your appearance is through your clothing. Many people want to live by the rule clothes do not **make** the man or woman. Although this is essentially true, that clothes do make perceptions of the man or woman. If you are unsure how well you are doing on this front, look around the office and see how you compare. A rule of thumb in dressing for success is to take your style cues from those two levels above you. You do not need to **spend** much money to present yourself well; you just need **to** take the time to care how others perceive you and, **more** important, how you see yourself. In the long run, you also want to ensure that your long-term physical characteristics are as pleasing as possible, too.

Although it may seem defeatist to bring this up in **the** context of a 90-day plan, individuals who feature negative physical characteristics such as bad teeth, excess **weight**, or bad skin will appear to many people as individuals who do not take care of themselves. These characteristics can, in some cases, be attributed to pure genetics. However, **it** is about perception. If you are afflicted with any of these **or** related characteristics, according to the rules of our culture you can expect that for the duration of your life these **sorts** of characteristics will be consistent reasons for others **to** judge you.

Like it or not, appearances will always come into play **when** others are judging your value, even when the characteristics have nothing to do with what you are being sized up for. If there is anything you can do to tend to these afflictions, you will eliminate that potential for poor judgment. In a perfect world this argument should not be made. If you plan on living in this world, you must recognize, and dismiss if you like, this practical advice.

We have touched a little on the importance of communication in exploring some of the messages we are sending and receiving, but that is only the tip of the iceberg. Everything is communication, and the next chapter will explore the matter more deeply.

Possible Pitfalls:

- Do not wallow in your flaws. Find a way to learn from or embrace them.

- Avoid blaming the messenger if the feedback you get from the people whom you ask opinions is hurtful to you.

- Express yourself through your appearance, but do not do so with a disingenuous gimmick.

- Disregard outside perceptions that do not apply to your plight for growth in the workplace.

- Keep yourself open to unexpected opinions that may help you to better understand perceptions people have about you.

CHAPTER 7

Communication

This week's checklist:

- Pay attention to how differently you speak to people who are subordinate to, equal to, and above you on the organizational tiers.

- Examine what forms of written communication you should improve and make a plan to do so.

- Choose one specific communication exchange in which you participate and take note of the context messages that have affected the exchange.

- Initiate a group discussion.

- Strike up a conversation with a higher-level employee.

Communication is commonly accepted to be the process for sending and receiving messages. In the broad sense, messages are sent and received unconsciously and with intent, through words and in context, by a multitude of channels.

The main channels we send messages are through our spoken words, written words, and the various dimensions of context that we use to communicate. These intentionally and unintentionally communicate messages attributable to us, and they influence or accent our other spoken or written messages. Often, these three means of communication (spoken, written, and context) work in conjunction to communicate the message we have intended. For example, telling a coworker you appreciate his hard work on your mutual project, then e-mail the boss to tell her this employee did a good job. Further interactions with this employee are surrounded by positivity, and the message of satisfaction is harmoniously pressed through all avenues of communication. At other times, however, these three modes of communication will do battle with each other. For example, telling a coworker you think he did a good job on your shared project but your facial expression tells him otherwise, it would be confusing. Then if you send him an e-mail expressing concern for some aspect of his work, the incongruity between modes of communication is confusing. These examples demonstrate how miscommunication may occur through sender error, but miscommunication through receiver error is common, too.

We communicate with intent, as is the case when we plan our words and specifically use them to communicate a purposeful message. However, the literal words we use can become distorted through the way we send them, the contextual cues that drown out our intended message, or through misinterpretations made by the receiver. Sometimes we choose words that do not end up on the receiving end the way we meant them, either through misinterpretation of our words or sender malfunction in which we sent an unclear or confusing message. For example, if you tell a coworker you thought he was doing a good job on Project A and he interpreted this as a surreptitious negative remark on his hard work on Project B, your intended message has become altered. Sometimes, an intended message may get muddled not through its verbal sending or the manner in which it is heard but through a contextual aspect that confuses its meaning. This can cause the message to come out twisted on the other end. This would be the case if, for example, an individual attempts to send a positive message and yet his or her facial expression gives the receiver the impression of a negative connotation.

Communication, as simple as it might feel to create and send a message, is ripe for bad results. Being mindful of the words you use, both in oral and written forms, will affect your chance of avoiding miscommunication. So, too, will taking into account the contextual messages that affect your intended messages or that serve to send messages on your behalf. There are also occasions you find yourself sending one message only to find that you had an ulterior motive, hidden even to yourself. For example, you believe you were spending extra attention on your boss's directions simply because you are a dutiful employee. Later on you may realize you were mulling over a potential favor and were trying to "butter him up." The media are often blamed for committing acts like this. According to some, media may share one message but subtly showcase a hidden agenda or the subtle stereotype. For example, a journalist may favor a public figure, and the adjectives she uses about him are positive in hue when they could be more neutral. The journalist could simply mention what the public figure had to say instead of mentioning he used "inspirational" words.

Sending and Receiving Messages

In examining your personal brand, we touched on some of the channels we use to send messages about ourselves and how they can be perceived. Our communication is not just bred through the words we use. It is also found in how we wield those words and when we choose to use them. It includes the facial expressions accompanying them, humor, clothing and accessories, technology, and more. Everything about you and everyone around you is involved in the process of sending and receiving messages. This is important to know, because it should give insight into why miscommunications are inevitable. It is also important to keep an open mind about what messages you are sending and receiving.

CASE STUDY: MATTHEW SMITH

Matthew Smith

Web site founder and operator

www.suburbanhorror.com

Organizations function on communication, yet good human communication is getting harder to find. Whatever happened to people communicating with people? At this point, I'd be willing to wait on hold for half an hour just to communicate with an actual person. Every time I call a business, a robot answers and tries to direct the call when all I want is to talk to a person! The worst is those robots that try to understand a human voice. No matter how clearly you speak they say, "Sorry, I did not understand your response." Then after a couple tries, instead of transferring you, they disconnect you.

I think not only would the world be a better place, but our lives would be easier if people just took the time to care and do things themselves. Instead of "making things easier," take the extra couple of minutes to deliver good customer service through human communication. I sort through around 300 e-mails a day from bands, labels, promotion companies, and freelance writers, and I do what I can to get back to each of them. Is it easy? No. Is it time consuming? Very much so. However, just by taking the extra couple of seconds to communicate with someone, I make that person's life easier, and that makes my life easier. Communicating with someone takes only a minute or two. Trying to get the person back on your side after ignoring him or her could take forever.

Speaking

Oral communication is one of the most common ways in which we communicate. We do it all the time. However, effective speech is difficult for many people, whether they realize it or not. How many times have you entered an argument over a simple miscommunication? It should be enough to say what we mean and be heard how we meant to say it. Yet, the reception of our messages can get lost in the muddle of sender error, receiver error, or contextual alterations. Also, through poor enunciation, hurried speech, stuttering, slang, accents, poor vocabulary, and more, our ability to speak our mind can become easier said than, well, said. Communication gaffes through speaking are plentiful and must be considered before they become a true hindrance to your advancement.

Ask yourself in which of these speaking situations you feel the most and least comfortable.

Interpersonal, Non-public Communication

Speaking with people one on one or in small, non-public settings is difficult for some people. For others, it is the only manner of speaking in which they feel truly comfortable. Consider how well your interpersonal communication episodes play out. If you believe you have experienced poor instances of interpersonal communication, evaluate what you may have done to contribute to the negative experience and consider the four main components to effective interpersonal communication.

First, all parties should be able to sufficiently send messages so the receiver(s) understand the sender's intent. Second, all parties should have the ability to receive the messages of the other person(s) and transmit the intended messages back correctly to demonstrate comprehension. Third, all parties must adhere to appropriate patterns of give and take in the conversation, by taking turns and discussing in equal measures. Fourth, all parties should recognize and express appropriate degrees of openness specific to their shared relationship(s).

Ignorance of these rules will lead to ineffective interpersonal communication. Adherence to these simple guidelines will assist in successful interpersonal communication. The process and this form of communication will become more easily managed, understood, and effective.

Public Speaking and Oratory Group Communication

In multiple surveys, respondents have implied public speaking is more frightening than even death. For example, in a poll conducted by the Dale Carnegie® Training program, the fear of public speaking ranked No. 1. According to a poll conducted by the Discovery Channel™, the only things more frightening than public speaking are acts that may very well lead to death, such as the fear of being buried alive or drowning. Phobias aside, speaking formally or informally in a public speaking arrangement or as the orator in a group communication setting may arouse stomach butterflies in many but need not be a terrifying experience. The purpose of public speaking is to share information, sometimes with the intention to sway, influence, or amuse. Experts suggest the typical cause for fear of public speaking is associated with the fear of appearing stupid. This fear can cause physiological responses, such as dry mouth, stuttering, shaking, and even heart palpitations, which can further hinder the ability to communicate effectively in this setting. Also, the fear of public speaking can lead to a self-fulfilling prophecy of sorts causing the speaker to, in effect, sound foolish due to the pressure associated with confronting the fear of public speaking. For the many people who fear public speaking, confronting their phobia is much easier said than done. Although getting past the fear of public speaking is especially daunting because one must do that which he or she is most afraid of, practice is the best way to assuage the fear. Public speaking coaches offer the following tips to diminish public speaking fears: prepare and practice, downplay the intimidation of your audience, and learn how to relax before speaking publicly. If you can find a way to tackle these nerve-wracking aspects of public speaking, you will become one of a valuable minority, a good public speaker.

Telephone Communication

Speaking via telephone seems simple enough, and yet this particular form of communication is quite troublesome for many individuals. A variety of reasons lend to these difficulties. For example, in some situations, telephone communication may feature the added dimension of anonymity. Studies indicate that when episodes of communication take place in some form of anonymity, typical rules of civil communication are often ignored. Additionally, the lack of visual cues in telephone communication can also alter the effectiveness of the exchange. In telephone conversations, face-to-face signals for such things as turn-taking and proper reception of message are absent, causing confusion for those who depend on those cues. To ensure effective episodes of telephone communication, the most important thing you can do is learn how to cater your telephone communication style to the dimensions of the medium. Recognize the limitations of telephone communication and adapt your communication to match those limitations. If you depend on visual cues in face-to-face communication, find another way in which to understand the flow of the telephone conversation. For example, ask open-ended questions to eliminate the fast-paced responses to yes and no questions. Attempt to adopt your telephone partner's pattern of speech so that you are more likely to match the pace of his or her communication. Summarize what the person has said so that it is clear you understand the information. Telephone communication can be a useful tool in the workplace, and for some it is vital. It may take work to discover the telephone communication methods that work for you, but when you figure them out, you will forever ensure effectiveness in this area of spoken communication.

Consider that most people have some insecurity in relation to one or all these means of oral communication. Your goal in effective oral communication is to get your intended message across as effectively and efficiently as you know how. If it is consistently getting lost along the way in any one of these vehicles of communication, all you can do is work on it. It may feel silly, but try having a talk with yourself in the mirror if you find interpersonal communication difficult. If group communication terrifies you, consider joining a public speaking club. If telephone speaking throws you for a loop, analyze what it is that is missing that throws off your game and then work to combat it.

Proficiency in oral communication stymies many, but our writing skills appear to be fading the most quickly. Many experts place some of the blame for this downslide in our writing skills on the influx of technological advances and our growing dependencies on information technologies and devices.

Writing

Technology waged a war on our writing skills long ago and has beaten the average person's understanding of writing to a bloody pulp. In the beginning, it was the spell check and grammar check that rendered the most damage. Our own attention to detail has slackened since these aides were made available. However, with these quick routes toward proofreading, the writer has less responsibility to learn how to spell well and properly apply grammar rules.

Spelling and grammar checks have been major culprits in this ongoing war against writing skills, but those particular shortcuts may be the least worrisome in the current vast army of warriors.

- Emoticons are unprofessional in the workplace.

- Instant- and text-message slang, with its lazy leanings toward typographic errors, allows us to say things more quickly but diminishes the quality of our typing and writing skills practice.

- Internet incivility, a modern-day phenomenon that is rampant and ever growing in intensity, is pervading the manner we use writing to communicate with one another. According to computer-mediated communication specialists, such as Susan Herring and J.T. Hancock, Internet communicators tend to express themselves with less civility than those in face-to-face episodes of communication. To some experts, this growing trend toward disinterest in and disregard to the rules of grammar and the new styles of written communication represent evidence of evolution. After all, language is always growing along with the times and needs of the culture it is used. These changes can be attributed to the development of more efficient and applicable means of communication. However, many communication specialists believe the overuse or improper use of these shortcuts and habits are evidence of inferior writing skills and indicate a downward trend for written communication.

These changes can be attributed to the development of more efficient and applicable means of communication. However, many communication specialists believe the overuse or improper utilization of these shortcuts and habits are evidence of inferior writing skills and indicate a downward trend for written communication and education. Additionally, the ugliness apparent In online communication degrades all forms of interpersonal communication. Whether the link is cause and effect or even simply a correlation, there has certainly been a rise in rudeness and a decrease in positive customer service in recent years.

The workplace is full of different forums for writing, and all types carry their own rules of protocol.

Memos

Memos are meant to convey a message to a group of individuals in a concise and efficient way. If a memo is bogged down with distracting infractions or missing essential components, the memo becomes just another nuisance. Three common problems of memo construction are wordiness, missing parts (headings, dates, sender), and good proofreading. Print and e-mail memos are a vital component to successful inter- and intraoffice communication, but if they are constructed poorly and have any one of the three common problems they can cast a shadow over impressions of you. Conversely, appropriate, proper, and efficient construction of successful memos will convey to others you are aware of what is important in the workplace, are willing to take the time to share information, possess good written communication skills, and are wise to the ways of efficient memo construction.

Reports

Every report written by you should be created with the complete care of a graduate-school thesis. If you have to create a document that will be shared by many people and that will likely be retained in the office files, it must be representative of your best work. It should be aesthetically appealing, with demonstrative charts and graphs as needed. It should be free of typos and embarrassing mistakes.

E-mails

E-mail communication has become an indispensable tool in business. Of course, with the good often comes the bad. Who has not committed at least one e-mail gaffe? Unintended "reply-all" responses, heat of the moment e-mail rebuttals, and unintentional neglect of time-sensitive communications are just a few that come to mind. There are many common-sense hard-and-fast rules that apply across the board: refrain from e-mailing customers or bosses in the laid-back manner you would enlist with your buddies; attaching heavy-duty, space absorbing documents without warning or request; and becoming too reliant on e-mail communication at the expense of more personal forms of communication, to name a few. Every organization's unofficial etiquette is different, so fashion your e-mail communication tendencies according to how the upper-level workers in your office conduct their e-mail communication. Delve into your files for some e-mails sent by the highest-ranking workers with whom you communicate, and add those rules to your repertoire. Of course, as with all other forms of written communication, show your best work so that no one can come to unfortunate conclusions about you.

Letters

Although letters are currently one of the least likely means by which you will communicate with colleagues, customers, and clients, there are still many instances in which paper letters are necessary and preferred. When a written record is necessary or if a special sentiment is being communicated, such as in a thank-you note, a letter is the way to go. As with all other forms of written communication, you do not want your letters to become muddled by mistakes. Appropriate headings; proper formatting with a greeting, body, and conclusion; and a thorough round of proofreading are all essential to good letter writing. Letters are appreciated for the personal touch they can give. Be wary, however, of providing too much of a personal touch in some situations. If handwriting a letter, think over your words carefully. Although letters can show someone you care enough to construct a letter just for them, if the tone of the letter feels too familiar people can become turned off.

Written forms of communication are a vital and useful means of exchanging messages in the workplace. With the opportunity, though, comes plenty of chances to come across less positively than you would like to present yourself. This is especially true now that you are trying to consistently show your employer your value to the company to secure a promotion. Pay attention to how you are presenting yourself in your workplace written communication.

The final area of communication we will examine, context messages, presents one more opportunity to show your best side as opposed to your possible deficiencies.

Context Messages

As we touched on briefly before, sometimes communication is imbedded not in the words we use, but in the context in which they are sent and received. Numbers vary, but experts suggest that the majority of communication is nonverbal. For example, Albert Mehrabian, a communication scholar, declared in the 1970s that words account for only 7 percent of our communication. Other sources, such as a prominent UCLA study, specify that approximately 93 percent of our communication is nonverbal. This means the words we use are often the least of our communication.

Consider all you take in when you enter a new environment: the colors of the walls, the setup of the furniture, the positions people take around the room, the clothes they are wearing, the aromas in the air, the time of day these people have congregated in this environment, the smiles, the frowns, the initiation of conversations, the cold shoulders, the bad breath, the raised eyebrows, and the proximity between people. Everything is involved in the swirl of messages.

The idea that an environment you have not personally constructed could send a message in your name might seem odd. However, consider this simple example:

You have prepared for three months to discuss promotion opportunities with your boss. You have taken every step to ensure you are fully prepared and feel confident in your chances of receiving the promotion you desire. However, on the day of your meeting a coworker has heated up a stinky casserole dish in the employee kitchen. The aroma is permeating the entire office, and during the course of the meeting with your boss, you can see the foul odor affecting her mood and, thus, quietly affecting her positive mood in your interactions.

Unfair as it may be, the alteration of the environment has affected your boss's perceptions of you and the outcome of your meeting. You have done nothing wrong, yet you suffer from the negative messages sent through the environment where you and your boss are interacting.

Obviously, you cannot control all aspects of your environment or instances of nonverbal communication, but you can certainly manipulate some portions to better affect your interactions.

Although nonverbal communication contains many different subsets and manifestations, the three categories that we will examine here are those most likely to affect how you are perceived at work. These are also the most open to your manipulation. We will cover the physical aspects of your communication, objects used in your communication, and the actions you take or do not take in and during your communication.

Physical

Physical communication is not only about how well you clean up. Certainly you communicate positive messages to your employer when you comb your hair, dress with care, and maintain a "no-body-odor" policy in the office. Yet, there are plenty of other ways you physically communicate that could be sending the wrong message to your boss. Simple acts such as facing your boss when she is speaking to you, maintaining eye contact, and attempting to sustain similar stature and presence are simple gestures that communicate attentiveness to your boss while denoting confidence in your position at work. Also, standing tall and straight, avoiding closed-off gestures such as folding your arms across your chest, and shaking hands with an appropriate blend of firmness without being too gentle will give others a positive impression of you, such as that you are confident and warm. Many other aspects of your physical presence can effectively send positive and negative messages. For example, overusing perfume can send a certain message. Also, a bad haircut or too much makeup may send the wrong message. Pay attention to the physical aspects of your presentation to understand how others might be nonverbally reading you. Tend to items that could be turning people off.

Objects

Objects are used in communication all the time, from the clothing and jewelry we wear to the decorative items we choose for our personal workplaces. In the workplace, one of the most common ways we use objects to communicate is in our personal workspace. Photos on your desk, personal items scattered about your area, and the books on your shelves say much about you. You should be mindful of what and how much you communicate through your personal workspace setting. Photos of your loved ones are fine. Photos of a loved one in a bikini may be a bit provocative and off-putting for your coworkers.

Consider the choices you have made in your workspace design. If you suspect you might be presenting yourself less favorably than you should through an unsavory screen saver, for example, make some changes that will communicate a more positive presentation. Any of your displayed personal or work-relevant objects or habits may be received as nonverbal communication. For example, your ever-present coffee cup could be "speaking" to others through its cleanliness, or lack thereof, the message emblazoned on its side, or even simply through its consistent position on one particular spot on your desk. Or, perhaps your tendency to twirl a strand of hair around a pencil as you speak could be communicating a particular message.

Actions

Your actions speak louder than words. You may say that you are committed to your job, but if your actions say otherwise, what will your boss believe? Many common actions can conflict with our assertions that we are good at, committed to, and prepared to move up in our jobs. Your actions will win out over your words every time. For example, arriving late to work, even by a couple of minutes, may say to your boss you are not committed to your job even as, through your verbal assertions, you say otherwise. Taking personal calls at work could suggest to your employer you do not value the money you earn during work hours. A promise that you will complete a project but submitting it late or doing a shoddy job on it screams that you have little concern for the job, the deadlines of the organization, or how you are perceived at work. Pay attention to those things you do that may be overshadowing your verbal communication. Do not simply say you are prepared to move up in the organization while you are showing your boss through your actions that this is not the case. You will look bad because you will seem disingenuous, and you will be caught demonstrating poor work habits that could hold you back.

Communication is the basis for all relationships and the processes of exchanging information. If you are mindful of all the messages you are communicating in your work relationships, you are more likely to have your intended messages heard and understood. Additionally, you will be better prepared to understand the messages sent to you from others. The next stop along your road will be a good test of your understanding of the many ways you can use effective communication to your advantage.

Possible Pitfalls:

- Pay attention to the context messages that affect your communication.

- Do not miss out on an opportunity to practice the form of communication you feel least comfortable.

- Work toward more professional communication in your workplace e-mailing.

- Take notice of the hidden-context messages other people are sending you.

- Proofread every item of written communication you create.

CHAPTER 8

Preparing Your Case

This week's checklist:
- Look over the goals you have set for yourself and improve them.

- Set aside time to prepare your case fully.

- Brainstorm all the potential roadblocks that could interfere with your goals.

- Clear your schedule adequately to allow for your upcoming meetings and any necessary time you will need for preparations.

- Get your expectations in check and identify three goals that are the most open to adaptations.

You have examined your work performance thus far and identified where you hope to rise in the future of your career, taken steps toward remedying issues that may have been holding you back, and have tried out some ideas that will help your job performance persona. Now is the time to start thinking about what you want from your promotion negotiations.

A good place to start is reviewing the goals you established for yourself in Week 2. When you wrote those goals, they should have been inspired by the zeal and unrelenting hope of someone who knows he or she deserves only the best. There is nothing wrong with lofty goals if you are prepared to put in the hard work that must come with attaining them. You know what you want, so start preparing your case for how you will get it.

If you took the advice and started archiving your work on a brag sheet, you will be instantly ready to prepare a case accented by the merit of your work history. Top managers have consistently expressed disdain for the entitlement displays of workers who expect they should be awarded a promotion for doing their job well. Promotions are not a prize to be won by the hardest-working, most deserved workers. Instead, promotions are offered as an incentive to those who have demonstrated productivity and promise, to entice them into higher positions to maximize their potential. The distinction is important and sheds light on how to begin preparing your case.

Looking back at what you have done so far for the company, you should be able to cite evidence of how you have done your job well and contributed to the goals of your workplace.

Keeping in mind that your upcoming promotion is not a reward for your positive work performance. In the absence of a fortune teller, history is the only proof your boss has to go by when forecasting your potential.

Begin your promotions discussion with a brief reference to some positive points in your work performance history. This will prepare your boss for the tone of your main discussion: what you hope to gain in your promotion. Your goal in preparing the presentation for your promotion meeting is to effectively communicate to your boss what exactly you want. In planning your case, you will want to prepare for the potential that your boss may have arguments against components of what you want. As well, you should arm yourself with ready compromises in case you need to settle on some points. First, before tackling the details of your promotion request and what aspects you may compromise, you must begin preparing the initial phase of the case you will present: evidence of your potential.

What Have You Done?

In the process of determining what you are capable of doing in the organization, your boss will look to what you have already done. In some cases, an individual's past experience can become the main focus in the process because, after all, what else does a boss have to go on besides concrete evidence of past success at work? Begin the discussion on your own terms, initiating the reference to the positive points in your work history.

If you have created a brag sheet, you will be ready to pull from the list a few ideas to bring up. But even if you have not yet specifically tracked your successes, you have spent weeks now examining the details of your work life and strengths. Thus, you have examined most aspects of what your value is to the workplace. Additionally, you have been improving what you do at work, so you are prepared to highlight demonstrations of those achievements. Now, you just need to produce usable evidence of it all to bring to the promotion- discussions meeting.

Reflect on what you have contributed to the workplace. Consider those aspects of the job where you have demonstrated your greatest strengths and aspects of what you regard as your personal brand. Feeling confident in your best qualities and what you have determined to be representative of who you are will allow you to proudly reflect on the contributions you reference at your meeting. Think of this aspect of the discussion as an informative orientation for your boss. Although he or she is likely aware of the details of your work history, starting the discussion with a refresher on what a good employee you have been will set the best stage for the rest of the discussion.

If possible, you should integrate references to successes that specifically translate the type of promotion you desire. If you can show your boss that you have already demonstrated the characteristics of the type of person who will be in the position you are requesting, he or she will be more likely to picture you in the role. For example, if you are in a position that has no ongoing managerial responsibility but the position you are requesting has some, consider how you may have demonstrated characteristics that would suggest you are capable of supervising others. Perhaps you can recall an example of how you demonstrated problem-solving skills on the job or a group project that you successfully headed.

Pull a few ideas from your work history that you believe will provide an excellent segue into detailing what you want in your promotion. Based on this starting point, begin consideration of what type of case you will be presenting to your boss and what method of preparation will be most advantageous for you.

Method of Preparation and Presentation

The manner you compile the relevant data and ideas for your presentation will depend on how you work best. Presenting your case successfully will be contingent on preparing a case that you feel confident presenting, consideration of how you believe your boss will best perceive your presentation, and, perhaps, the presentation formats that are typical to your industry, workplace, and personal creativity.

For the meeting you will want to have a reference list of your personal successes in the organization. You may not need to consult it, but if you do, you should attempt to do so without giving the impression that you are reading a list. But you should prepare this list, based on the aforementioned examination of citing evidence of your positive work history so that you can bring it to the meeting with you. You will appreciate having it if even for the simple reason of comfort. There, in the meeting right by you, it will be a cheerleading team of all that you have been able to accomplish so far.

If you feel comfortable doing so and it seems appropriate to the meeting, you could even prepare a meeting agenda handout starting with brief reference to your successes to accent your claims and impress your boss with your creativity, organization, and resolve. As well, creating a one-page handout will provide assistance to your talking points and guide your boss through your presentation. It will not take long to whip up a professional-looking diagram of, for example, what monies you have pulled into the organization from various projects. In the end you may not use the explanatory material you compile to defend your case, but over-preparedness is a good thing in this case. Your mind should be swimming with those reasons why you have been a valuable employee and how your work history suggests your potential for the promotion you are requesting.

Although you should be prepared with helpful outlines or lists, you may choose to plan your presentation more loosely, without a handout or a specific structure. Some people work better in this situation if they treat it as a conversational exchange of information and ideas. If you believe this is how you work, your best bet may be to stay away from too much structure. You will still want to have a complete plan for what ideas you will want to present, but your preparation and practice may consist of practicing a hypothetical dialogue between you and your boss as opposed to preparing for a presentation where your ideas are expressed through a monologue or a meeting led more directly by you.

In addition to considering the methods of presentation, you might incorporate determining what exactly you want from the promotion.

What Exactly Do You Want?

When you created your three-month goals, as specific as you might have been, you may have focused on the obvious and specific things like a raise in money and power. Perhaps you specified the exact monetary increase you expected and the exact title you planned on getting along with the raise, but there is so much more to consider when asking for a promotion. Your aim in preparation for presenting your case is to refer to those initial goals and expand them. Consider everything you could possibly hope to gain in this promotion, and begin sifting through all those options for what matters to you most and what you should expect to have access to.

In Week 2, when the topic of miswants was covered, perhaps you reconsidered why you want what you want. You took a new perspective, determining different types of goals than you would have originally thought you would want to achieve. Or, maybe you felt justified and comfortable with your desires and were ready to continue your promotion request planning based on those original desires. Either way, do not limit your negotiations to the bare bones of a promotion. Money and power are obvious, though certainly beneficial, expectations of a promotion. However, there are plenty of other perquisites you should consider that could be just as valuable to you in the long run.

Think about the possible perks that could be integrated into your promotion package.

- Depending on your field, setting, or position, payment of car or cellular phone costs could reap the same financial advantages as a monetary raise. Even though you most likely use these items for personal use as well, if you use them for work purposes repayment of those costs would be an understandable bonus to your bottom line.

- The ability to work from home a specific number of days a month is another popular option. So, too, are the options of flex time or extra vacation days. These possibilities are contingent on many factors, of course, and should never be seen as an opportunity to lighten your overall work load. In terms of work and life balance, though, being granted any of these privileges could be extremely rewarding, even beyond financial gains.

- Requesting permission to attend a specific number of job-relevant seminars or working vacations may be a double benefit. Being allowed this occasional deviation from your regular days can be both educational and an enjoyable change of pace. As well, asking for this privilege demonstrates to your boss the commitment you have to furthering your skill set and work performance.

- Although it may seem sadomasochistic to ask for more work without specific dollars attached, requesting access to a higher-profile project could be the best thing for your career. It may lead to a higher position on completion, more pay in the long run, and more admiration from higher-ups.

Create the perfect but appropriate job description and benefits package you feel you are prepared. List every aspect of the plan and consider this your point of attack as you determine your promotion request plans. You will also want to determine what you will be willing to settle for.

What Will You Settle For?

The goal in your promotion negotiations is to win over your boss and get everything you want. Achieving this goal is a definite possibility. There is every reason to believe that, if you have considered every angle of the potential of a person in your position and with your skill level, education, and work history, you will get what you want. Sometimes, though, there are things you have not considered, do not know about, or that are out of your control. It is for these reasons that you must consider, before going in to present your case, what you are willing to compromise.

Imagine the worst possible reaction to your request. Maybe you are greeted with absolute contempt, uncomfortable stonewalling, or a boss who is insulted by even the mere suggestion that you are not completely and absolutely grateful for being allowed admittance into the building.

Requesting a promotion can be intimidating to many people due to the fear they will be embarrassingly shot down or, worse yet, lose their jobs for bringing it up. However, you have every right to request a promotion, and it is highly unlikely that requesting a promotion will contribute or lead to your termination. These are not concerns that should hold you back from getting your promotion.

What is a realistic possibility is that you will not be instantly handed every item on your list. You may need to sell yourself a bit and be willing to compromise. If you do not have all angles of the promotion process considered or receive an unexpectedly poor reception to your request, your place in the organization could become jeopardized for reasons you may not have considered. How are you going to feel if you are expecting a promotion but end up with nothing because you were not fully prepared for compromising? You need to have a back-up plan: Know exactly what you will settle for and what exactly you will do if you are dissatisfied with your results.

From your list of promotion expectations, put them in order of what you absolutely must gain to what you can live without. Then, assign each a number value from one to ten to have a way to compare them against each other. Your top priority may score a ten and represent the one item that you must attain. Your bottom two priorities may be completely expendable, or you may end up factoring them in as matters of compromise. For example, if your second-place priority is fairly important to you but is something that your boss is not able or willing to include in your promotion, you may be satisfied with lower-valued compromises that, together, benefit you just as much as your second-place priority would have.

CHAPTER 8: PREPARING YOUR CASE

Your promotion discussions are a negotiation. Start out strong with everything you hope to get and then some. Work from there to get those items that will satisfy you and make you feel that you have found success through this process. Know ahead of time what specifically those details are. Consider a variety of formulas:

- I will accept a promotion that includes Priorities A, B, and C.

- I will accept a promotion that includes a variation on Priorities A and C if E and F are included in full.

- I will not accept a promotion that does not include Priority A.

Think of every variation of what you will and will not accept as a promotion plan. Clarify fully what will happen if you do not get the minimum of what will satisfy you. If you are unhappy with the results, without a forward-thinking plan you are likely to grow dissatisfied with your job. The outcome of your not getting what you want does not have to be anything drastic like quitting your job or staging a revolt on the premises. What could be most beneficial to your career would be using the process to figure out how to be successful the next time around.

Even if you do not get everything you had hoped for or even anything, turn the meeting into a positive experience by treating it as a reconnaissance mission. Be prepared to take many notes because now is your boss's turn to tell you specifically what you need to do to move up. If your boss does not think you are ready for a promotion, you have every right to kindly request his or her recipe for getting there. However, do not be surprised if he or she does not supply it.

Being prepared for the worst scenario will help you to specifically define what your priorities and expectations are, but before you get to the point where you could be denied, you should beat your boss to the punch. Come up with preemptive counterarguments ahead of time to deter your boss from finding excuses to refute your requests.

Coming Up with Preemptive Counterarguments

For every pro there is a con, and your boss may well be the con master. Play the role of devil's advocate ahead of time before falling into this trap during your negotiations. A good way to prepare is through a pro-and-con exercise. You do not want to leave anything up to chance or not be prepared, so thwart the objections before they are even submitted.

Make a pros list of all the reasons why you should get everything you want from your promotion. Cite specific evidence from your work history to substantiate your claim, brainstorm good ideas that you could use in your new position, and think up specific ways in which you are capable of contributing due to being given the things for which you are asking.

When you have exhausted your list of pros, create a list of possible cons. Take the perspective of your boss and consider what he or she might consider a con in relation to your job change. For example, people often get passed up for promotions due to a simple comparison of costs versus benefits. Write down all the possible reasons that your boss might perceive your promotion as a bad deal for the organization. This may include some references to your known weaknesses, but more relevant would be the circumstantial reasons that giving you what you want could be costly to the company. For example, you want one telecommuting day a month, but it could cause jealousy in the office and pestering requests from other employees to be given the same right.

Now that you have a pros list and a cons list, focus on one more. For every single con, create a counterargument. For example, if you recognized that your boss might see finding someone to fill your old position as a potential cost to the organization, your counterargument may be that you have been working closely with just the right person and have even shown him or her around the workings of your job. Even if your boss does not approve of your suggestion, he or she will likely appreciate that you took the initiative to control this potential cost. Ultimately, of course, you have no say in who should move up in the workplace, but this sort of forward thinking will reflect positively on you even if you do not squash the concern.

If you are faced with the opportunity and need to supply a counterargument, simply offer your suggestion without being pushy. This is not literally an argument. You should not feel entitled to persuade your boss against every protestation. But you should feel comfortable engaging in a friendly debate for which you have prepared yourself. For more information on preparations for counterarguments, please consult Chapter 13.

Having prepared your case and considered the potential hurdles that may curtail your efforts, the last step in your preparations is in taking a careful look at how your expectations factor into the process.

Expectations

Optimism is a funny thing. On the one hand, studies show that a positive attitude can lead to self-fulfilling prophecies. If you expect to get what you want, you are more likely to attain it. In reference to your goal of getting a promotion, this could be true in good part because when you expect to get a promotion you act in such a way as to create the fulfillment of that expectation. In this case, you may work harder up until the point in which you request your promotion, or you may take greater care to prepare your promotion request more thoroughly and thoughtfully.

On the other hand, optimism unaccompanied by the hardworking actions needed to propel you toward your goals is just blind faith. Simply expecting that you will get what you want, but not doing anything to manifest your goals, will get you nowhere. You can convince yourself that you have contributed so much to the organization that it would be crazy not to give you everything you demand, but if you cannot demonstrate this to your boss through hard work on the job or through a well-designed promotion presentation, it is unlikely that you will get the promotion you want, with or without extraordinary optimism.

Do not expect to succeed just because you want it so much, have faith that good things are coming your way, or feel entitled for any reason. Your expectations need to be insured with hard work, a thorough understanding of yourself and the organization, and a well-conceived, thoroughly planned attack. Be optimistic in your expectations but realistic. Ultimately, with good planning, hard work, and realistic expectations, you will guide yourself to success in your career. However, you must be grounded to control that ascent.

You have a plan of attack and have taken into account various aspects that could hinder the process. Your next step is in preparing the specific details of the meeting: who, what, where, and when.

Scheduling the Meeting

You are about to approach your last month of preparations. Scheduling the meeting a full month in advance is not always necessary, but you will want to start planning now for the specifics of the meeting. For example, you may need to schedule one or more brief consultations with a supervisor to solidify a better understanding of company policies. You may want to pencil in a casual, pre-negotiations talk with your boss to let him or her know of your plans for the larger discussion. Of course, giving consideration to your boss's busy schedule and planning a meeting with a comfortable cushion of distance into the future makes you look good.

In determining the specific details of the meeting, you should consider if anyone other than your immediate boss will be present. You can consult someone in human resources or the company guidelines to get your answer. Or, you could simply ask your boss for the protocol typical for this process in your organization. Requesting this information from your boss will also provide a good segue to some pre-negotiations banter.

In addition to determining who should be present at the meeting, you should also determine details regarding what this process typically looks like in the organization and where it usually takes place. For example, you may discover that your boss would prefer you meet on multiple occasions with various personnel or that the meeting should take place at a restaurant as opposed to the workplace. Also, you should be able to establish a standard timeline for the meeting or meetings that will take place. Typically, a meeting of this sort should take between a half-hour and one hour, but this will vary depending on the organization's practices and the preferences of those involved. Find the answers to all of these questions so you do not diminish your chances based solely on deviations from protocol.

You will also need to figure out the best time to schedule the meeting. Depending on who will be present, consult their calendars first and foremost. You should present yourself as accommodating rather than give anyone the impression that you do not value his or her time. Ask first when would be a suitable time and, then, work it in with your schedule as obligingly as you are able while still attempting to schedule at a time that will be most advantageous to your chance for success (more on the timing of your meeting in Chapter 9).

CHAPTER 8: PREPARING YOUR CASE

Every person is unique and will handle situations according to his or her own specific personality, but it is possible to learn enough details about the person or people with whom you will be discussing your promotion to heighten your chance of success. Additionally, you can expect most upper management types to possess certain characteristics and can use those generalities to your advantage. Before meeting with the person or people who will be deciding the fate of your promotion, increase your chance for success by getting to know the employer, boss, manager, or supervisor who will be reviewing your case.

Possible Pitfalls:

- Do not over-prepare the data you will be incorporating into your presented case. This is not a soliloquy.

- Ensure that your goals are clearly defined.

- Make sure you have determined compromising points.

- Clarify every potential angle of defeat that might threaten your case.

- Do not give your boss or any other participating person the impression that you do not value his or her time as you go about scheduling your meeting.

CHAPTER 9

Employers, Bosses, Managers, and Supervisors

This week's checklist:

- Take a closer look at who your boss is as a person and not just as a supervisor.

- Adopt a positive attitude, if you have not already.

- Find or create an opportunity in which to demonstrate your leadership skills.

- Pay attention to your boss's schedule and determine when and on what days he or she will most likely react positively to your promotion request.

- Assess your level of productivity and determine a strategy to improve upon it.

Throughout this book, employers, bosses, managers, and supervisors have been referenced due to the important part they play in your workplace experience. They have influence over the employees under their management, as their significance is often multifaceted. They may, at different times, assume different positions in your work life: mentor, bully, motivator, intimidator, teacher, leader, and comrade. The influence of each of these roles may affect who you are in the workplace, and definitely, these are the people who will be the gatekeepers to your future in the organization.

For the sake of simplicity, from here on, the person (or people) who fills the important position above you will be referred to as your boss. Each role is different, of course, but for the purpose of discussing these people in reference to your plan to get a promotion, understanding how they factor into your efforts will essentially be the same for each.

Countless popular characters present workplace bosses in a rather unflattering light. Stereotypical bosses abound. The octogenarian Mr. Burns from *The Simpsons*™ typifies the heartless boss. There is the clueless boss, like Michael Scott of TV's *The Office*. Donald Trump™, a supposedly real person who nevertheless seems the most contrived character of all, represents pompous bosses everywhere. Of course, we cannot forget cult film classic *Office Space*'s Bill Lumbergh personifying all three horrible traits: heartlessness, cluelessness, and pomposity.

Although these stereotypes are certainly exaggerated versions, the ideas come from somewhere, and it can be assumed that the characters' creators may have stolen from their own personal experiences with real-life bosses. Indeed, we all have stories of bosses whose character, judgment, qualifications, personal hygiene, or sanity we could bring into question. These sorts of incongruities caused me to constantly question who this seemingly crazy person was.

Bosses, like all people, are complicated creatures. As sociologically aware as you may claim to be, you cannot assume to completely understand the complexity and instability of human behavior. However, you can do some research to understand your boss enough to better your chance for growth at work. You can actively learn more about your boss to understand what you should do to improve the odds that he or she will favorably perceive your promotion request. Additionally, you can learn more about typical bosses, through research-based theories, to up your chances as well. For example, according to syndicated workplace columnist Anita Bruzzese, bosses are often swayed toward workers who consistently make them, the bosses, look good. Also, most bosses tend to be more receptive to employee requests during certain times of the day and week. Putting your personal research together with the ideas presented here will give you an edge in understanding how you can most advantageously pursue your promotion.

Learning more about your boss and his or her behaviors will certainly illuminate those boss behaviors that have baffled you in your past, but still do not assume you can learn enough to manipulate him or her. Take this information and learn from it. One thing you can be assured of is that your boss is above you on the organizational food chain for a reason. Although the reasons may not be applicable to your quest to rise up, your boss will always have something to teach you because, after all, he or she has reached at least one of your goals first. To learn from your boss, first you must try to understand him or her (or, at least, understand the parts that can help you).

Understanding Your Boss

Understanding another human being is no small feat. If the reverse were true, the American divorce rate would not be so high. People can spend decades of their lives with spouses and still feel as though they do not know each other. Do not expect to delve into the deepest crevices of your boss's mind. Be content with coming out the other end of this experience with simply a better knowledge of how your boss got to where he or she is today, what his or her day-to-day work experience looks like, and what types of behaviors and characteristics he or she appreciates in peers and underlings.

One of the key components of attempting to better understand your boss is tuning into your empathetic side. Empathy, for some people, is so strong that they may physically feel the pain of others. Yet, for many, it is severely lacking. If you are the type who tears up during a particularly sappy greeting card commercial, use that tendency to your advantage and entertain the idea of walking in your boss's shoes. If not, put on your empathy trainers and start out with some baby steps.

Pay close attention to your boss this week, while keeping it casual. To understand what your boss is looking for in promotable employees, you need to gain a better understanding of who he or she is in the workplace, how he or she ended up as a boss, and what he or she appreciates in other employees. One way to find these facts is through simple conversation.

When the time feels right, if you do not already know the details, engage your boss in a conversation about his or her rise up at work. How did he or she end up in the high-level position? Did he or she have any relevant jobs in other organizations first? If you have a reasonably comfortable relationship, try bringing up admirable peers or bosses about whom your boss might have insight. You certainly do not want to be gossipy. Instead, make a comment on an individual who you believe your boss likes as a professional or whom you have admired yourself. Any positive discussion with your boss on others at work will be a boon to your mental database of promotion-relevant knowledge.

A distanced observation of your boss will, as well, help you to figure out further usable details. Pay attention to your boss's communication style, what types of patterns he or she follows in conducting regular business, and with which employees your boss chooses to engage. Every seemingly minor detail of your boss's day could bring you one step closer to understanding the person who will either be deeming you worthy or unworthy of a promotion. Take every detail about your boss into consideration.

Anything you can observe about your boss may contribute to your cause. Mentally take note of how your boss acts in a variety of settings and in relation to different situations. Examine how he or she tends to communicate with others, in group settings, and in written documents. Pay attention to how your boss dresses when trying to impress. Consider the types of projects your boss undertakes and how he or she approaches and completes the related tasks. Through simple observations, you can garner a good deal of useful information. Remember, though, the point is not to recreate yourself into your boss's "mini-me. The point is to learn how to speak your boss's language so you can figure out how best to communicate your request and be rewarded with positive results.

Understanding your boss is vital to creating a successful promotion plan, but enlisting useful information about bosses in general may be just as helpful and leaves less to your subjectivity. In the end, your boss's behavior may not be explained through these general theories. However, using this data in your quest to understand the workings of your boss will, at least, open your exploration up to a variety of new possibilities and ideas. For example, employees who possess the skill of making their boss look good are perceived well in the workplace, especially by their boss.

The Skill of Making Your Boss Look Good

Studies show that most bosses favor those employees who make them look good. There are two main reasons they appreciate this quality. First, your boss may have the desire to be reviewed favorably just as you do. Thus, if your boss can find an employee who is able to assist him or her in that goal, your boss would appreciate the employee. That is, although your boss may not feel the need to prove to anyone else that he or she is a successful manager, your boss may be partial to the employees who are most manageable because they make the office machine run more smoothly with less oversight.

Consider how your boss strives to be perceived in the workplace. Just as you want to make a good impression on your boss, your boss too may have people he or she wants to impress. Whether your boss's audience is the company owner or the clientele your organization serves, part of your lasting impression on your boss may lie in your ability to make him or her look good. Contributing to this end should not be perceived as an act of "kissing up." It is your job, after all, to work toward the objectives of your boss's management. Therefore, if you do your job well, your boss can do his or her job well, and everyone looks good.

Your boss wants his or her workplace to be successful and will appreciate your efforts toward that goal. This, too, should be your goal, whether you want to get in good with the boss or not. You are part of an organization. For the system to succeed, it is essential the parts function productively and efficiently together. If you make every effort to follow the lead established by your boss, you will not only make your boss look good, but yourself as well.

In working toward making your boss look good, for whatever reason, there are some things you should consider doing and some things you should consider not doing. For example, the skill of making your boss look good is not about talking him or her up in front of peers or complimenting your boss's impeccable wardrobe every time he or she shows up in new garb. These sorts of behaviors can ring disingenuous if you are doing them solely for the reason of trying to win over affection. Instead of coming up with ideas to persuade your boss that you have the skills to make him or her look good, simply focus on doing your job well so that you do make your boss look good. **Do your job to the best of your ability so you can help create for your boss a highly functioning and productive workplace.** If you want to make your boss look good, strive to be the cohesive element in your office.

Being the glue that keeps the place together is a lofty enterprise, but if you are capable it can be rewarding. This type of employee is the go-to person, the one who your boss knows to trust for the correct information, completion of tasks, and for a positive attitude. Do your research regularly so when your boss needs an answer from the staff you have it. Also, stay away from petty office politics, and instead be the peacekeeper and leader in the office. Be the person who can solve problems and maintain harmony. Additionally, do not fill the air with meaningless efforts. You will not fool anyone if you are simply pretending to be the office glue. Be the person with thoughtful questions, the sort of thought-provoking queries that help everyone, including your boss, to consider all angles of the operation.

Another aspect to consider if you want to be the type of employee who can skillfully make your boss look good is how well you can keep the office communication avenues flowing. E-mailing peers and your boss on happenings, problems, and efficiency issues in the office that pertain to them or projects you work on together will keep everyone in the loop and aware that you are contributing to your boss's goals of maintaining a harmonious, productive office. Maintain professional relationships with everyone involved in your boss's operations so that you can continuously assist in maintenance of the office's communication.

In addition to the research that indicates the average boss's affinity for employees who make him or her look good, studies show there are other specific traits that most bosses routinely appreciate and look for in promotable employees.

CASE STUDY: RIKKE ALDERSON

Rikke Alderson

Senior Director

Brand Management

DoveBid, Inc.

In the course of my career, I have worked in public relations, advertising, media, politics, and electronics. I started out in receptionist roles and have since climbed as far as senior director, my current position.

Understanding the dynamics of boss and employee relations can contribute to promotion-related goals. Individuals who possess characteristics that help them to navigate relationships with superiors successfully are the types of people who get promoted. For example, an individual who can get her boss to appreciate the superior contributions she has made to the organization is skilled in this area. So, too is the employee who has a talent for making his boss look good. If an individual is able to give senior executives the impression that she can make their lives easier or make them look better, she will successfully create opportunities in her career.

Remember, a can-do attitude goes a long way, but there is a fine line between being taken advantage of and contributing to the goal of getting a promotion. If you have not risen to a higher level in three to five years, depending on the industry, you should move on and find other opportunities for growth.

Traits Supervisors Look for in Promotable Employees

Yes, all bosses are different, but there are certain traits that most of them tend to look for in promotable employees.

Workplace studies vary slightly in answers, but there are some commonalities between typical responses made by bosses across the board.

Three statistically stand out right up top and are characteristics you should adopt immediately regardless of whether you have specifically noted your boss's favor for these traits. Each one will benefit you whether your boss notices one or not. According to the research, bosses like employees with a positive attitude who show leadership skills and who demonstrate productive efficiency.

Demonstrating a positive attitude can come in many forms. Some might imagine a positive attitude as something a motivational speaker might posses and feel that an overstated can-do attitude is just not a part of their character. Luckily, this is a misconception. The last thing the world and your office needs is a phony character. You will not get ahead if you are just playing a part that you think others see when they imagine success. Being fake will set you back.

Instead, consider what a positive attitude is and is not. A positive attitude is not about being happy go lucky, chipper, and bouncy (unless that is your genuine self, of course). Demonstrating a positive attitude is about showing up for work eager to start the day with the preparedness to do the job to the best of your abilities. It is about taking on an assignment, or offering to be in charge of an assignment, with the excited zeal of opening an unknown present. A positive attitude is about possessing an energy that is enjoyable to be around, contagious to others, and shows you are happy to be at work, eager to learn, and optimistic that life and work is full of opportunities around every corner. Your boss is drawn to people like that, so tap into that side of yourself and let it shine through. Life is good and work is full of exciting opportunities. You are eager to explore the day before you every time you enter your workplace.

Good leadership is another trait that you should attempt to adopt immediately. Without leadership, things simply just do not get done. So it makes sense that bosses are always on the lookout for indications of strong leadership. It is a quality that some may feel they possess naturally, although others may not have the confidence, initiative, or skills it takes to enact good leadership. The lucky thing is that leadership is something that builds on itself, and all it takes to get that snowball rolling is demonstrating it once.

Most people do not want to be in charge of making a decision, despite the fact they may recognize the value of strong leadership. But being responsible for making a decision brings with it the liability of being accountable for the decision and the possibility of failure. So why bring that on when, instead, a person could just sit back and let some other person take the blame and chance at making a mistake? But consider that this process is all about your move up, and those at the top, inevitably, must lead those at the bottom. Therefore, the only way to hone the leadership skills you will have to demonstrate at the top is to practice them now before you get there. It is well worth the risk of liability and failure to gain experience that will lend to the higher positions ahead of you, especially because enacting the traits of leadership now will also get you there more quickly.

Considering that the bottom line of business is about productivity, it makes sense that upper managers would name efficient productivity as a top trait to look for in promotable employees. Accordingly, the person who produces succeeds. But just being productive will not necessarily get you anywhere if no one sees it. To get noticed as someone who is productive, you need to be an ongoing model of efficient productivity, not just a part-timer. Being productive is the goal of your job, but producing efficiently should be the highest goal of all you strive for.

Previously, we examined how much time is wasted at work, and this point is especially poignant in consideration of your productivity. People love a good excuse and will always have ready reasons to slack off; justifications for laziness are easy to come by. But in being your own boss and keeping vigilant watch over all that you are doing, you will find there are no reasons to slack off. There is always work to be done, even if you have to go out of your way to find it, invent it, or create a situation in which there is something to be done for the organization. It is easy to lose focus when you do not have a clear agenda for your day. Always have a list of tasks you must get done on each given day, some that can be tackled any time and some that contribute to the organization but are superfluous to the guidelines of your job. You are being paid to work for the organization, so you should always be working. Continuous, efficient production will be noticed.

Having considered what your boss is looking for in a good employee, you should also mull over the most obvious way in which you may boost your odds: hitting the right time to discuss your promotion. Experts have a few ideas when that might be.

What Days and Times of Day Are Best to Ask for a Promotion

You may not have the chance to pick and choose when your promotion will take place. Your boss's schedule is likely full, your calendar may also be tight, and, if anyone else is expected to take part in the process, you must consider his or her calendar as well. However, if presented with the opportunity to choose, take full advantage of this fantastic break. A 2000 study reported In the New Mexico Business Journal suggests that your meeting will have a greater chance for success if you choose the right day of the week and time of day. It is not a perfect science, but if your boss's workweek looks like most, statistically, the best day and time to discuss a promotion may be Thursday afternoon.

Through analysis of typical Monday through Friday workweeks, researchers have observed patterns that can help employees predict what day of the week to schedule a meeting with their boss to get the best results. Multiple variables must interplay to mark this day as the best choice. Extraneous items also can alter the formula. Therefore, when considering what day to schedule your meeting, you should do some sleuthing on your own first. Take into account your own observations of how your boss conducts his or her week. Observe your boss to determine whether you can detect a pattern for when he or she is in the best and worst moods. As well, consider the typical incidents of your boss's regular week and the out-of-the-ordinary incidents that will be occurring around the days you are considering.

In lieu of any strong observations regarding your boss's schedule, habits, and happenings, follow advice such as that listed in the *New Mexico Business Journal©* study. Accordingly, the report notes that the beginning portion of the week, Monday and Tuesday, is usually reserved for playing catch-up after the weekend and tending to negative employee business. Managers tend to focus on the negative business at the start of the week to allow for fine-tuning of the changes through the rest of the week. Thus, Monday and Tuesday are likely not the best days to expect thoughtful, positive attention to your plight; too much attention is already being used for housecleaning. The tail end of the week, Friday, is allotted for wrapping up business before the weekend and is also used to prepare for the upcoming week after the weekend. Therefore, Friday is not the best day to schedule a meeting with your boss because he or she is likely to be consumed with time-sensitive tasks. This leaves mid-week, Wednesday and Thursday. Wednesday, although a good potential choice, is second to Thursday because your boss may still be riding the hump of mid-week attention to pressing tasks. Thursday, however, often feels more relaxing to people because they can feel the weekend almost coming and yet they have not been fully confronted with the pressure of getting everything done before the workweek ends. Therefore, Thursday is likely to be the most advantageous time for you to schedule a meeting with your boss so that he or she will feel most relaxed and be able to focus on what you have to say.

The time of day you schedule your meeting also can affect its outcome. Research shows that, on any typical day, the flow of the average boss's day will also tend to follow a pattern. Just as in consideration of which day of the week you should schedule the meeting for the best results, selecting the best time of day is dependant on a variety of factors specific to your boss's typical schedule, habits, and happenings. Thus, first, you should consider your boss's personality when determining the best time of day to schedule your meeting. For example, take into account observances on such things as your boss's eating habits. If you notice that your boss is most content during the morning's café latte but hits a bad mood around 11 a.m., when the caffeine has worn off and lunch has not yet arrived, factor that pattern into your planning. Pay attention to everything about how your boss carries through the typical day to determine if there is anything that could be applicable to your cause.

If you are not quite sure what time of the day will be best regarding your particular boss, then consider what the experts have to say. According to various studies, the morning is seen as the time of the day when people are most energetic. This may be problematic to your cause as that energy is funneled into tunnel-vision productivity. Interfering with that flow of productivity can be a subconscious threat to those desires, even if you have a planned meeting with your boss, and may negatively affect your boss's feelings toward you and your plight. The hours in the late afternoon are, like the latter part of the week, reserved for wrapping things up. That late in the day, then, is not the most advantageous time for your cause. The early afternoon soon after lunch, however, is a near-perfect time. Just like that Thursday slide down to more relaxed feelings, the early afternoon impresses on people that it is time to start winding down. Studies show that blood pressure begins lowering for the average person at this point in the day. If your boss feels more relaxed and less pressed for time, he will be more likely to devote quality time to the efforts of examining your potential.

Again, pinpointing the best day and time to schedule an appointment to discuss your promotion is not an exact science and can vary wildly on the schedule and tendencies of your boss. Therefore, observe your boss's weekly and daily patterns to get an idea of what time and day are ideal for your specific situation. Ultimately, you may have to take what you can get. So do your best to plan well, but do not worry too much if you cannot control this aspect of your meeting. Focus on those things you know you have power over.

Understanding your boss will benefit you in your quest for a promotion and your experience in the organization . However, the relationships with your coworkers must be nurtured, too. Because these types of relationships may require more regular interaction, they may need even more attention to function smoothly and effectively for you.

Possible Pitfalls:

- Do not give your boss the impression that you are kissing up to him or her.

- Do not treat your boss like an equal colleague.

- Do not assume that you know the details of your boss's job and, instead, learn more about what he or she does.

- Never take the opportunity to belittle your boss.

- Never miss an opportunity to make your boss look good.

CHAPTER 10

Coworkers and Network Associates

This week's checklist:

- Get to know the people who work with you.

- Find outside opportunities for networking.

- Practice conflict management skills with a trusted friend.

- Brainstorm for potential mentors.

- Assess the dynamics of office politics in your organization.

Organizations can provide tricky environments. They are composed of a variety of different personalities who are stuck together all day long, day after day and expected to operate as a unit. As anyone who has ever had a roommate can attest, getting along with other people for an extended number of hours is not always easy. Often, it can feel downright impossible.

Obviously, playing well with others is an ability that applies far beyond preschool. Just as past teachers may have instructed, do unto others as you would have others do unto you, and you should be able to manage a relationship with even the most trying coworker. You cannot expect to enjoy everyone, but you should strive for being the type of person who can keep the peace as much as possible. This is something that will set you apart in the typical sea of disharmony and disagreeableness.

In addition to being seen as the type of person who is amiable and can get along with just about anyone, keeping your days drama free and void of unnecessary conflict will make work more enjoyable. Although many people seem to thrive on the ups and downs of bad blood in the office, if you asked the average person whether he or she would choose to spend their days fighting with others, few people would willingly select to work that way. Yet, so many offices are laden with battling coworkers.

The laws of office politics guarantee that, during any given time, at least one pair of your coworkers will be in the midst of some type of clash. Sometimes it may feel as if you have been transported back to junior high school, with the cliques, cold-hearted acts of exclusion, and the drama. Yet, as with any large conglomeration of different personalities, the occasional (or, in some cases, frequent) onslaught of friction is inevitable. Caged up in an office setting, the eventuality of stir-crazy strife among people is to be expected.

When confronted by conflict, the best choice for your career and your peace of mind is to put aside your pride and judgment of the crazy behaviors others exhibit. Look at conflict as an opportunity to enact your star-quality communication skills. Be your own mediator and work toward deciphering the point of view of the individual you are experiencing conflict with. Handling inevitable instances of conflict is all about being able to take a step back from the action and make the appropriate choices for a comfortable, all-pleasing solution. Honing your empathetic side will benefit that effort.

Empathy, the ability to walk in another person's shoes, is a characteristic high on the list of every supervisor's wants for employees and a trait that will help you learn more about yourself and humanity. Open-mindedly observing the behaviors around the office will serve you well. At times you will find that people can do crazy things for crazy reasons. Other times, you will see that people can do crazy things for sane reasons. But, it may be those times you discover yourself doing the craziest things that will be the most valuable of all. In the heat of battle, the view looks different, and sometimes, we surprise even ourselves by the mindless tactics we enlist to pay back others for behaviors we do not like. Catch yourself behaving badly, and you will learn much about yourself and humankind.

The relationships you have with coworkers and people in your organization's broad network are the mainstay of your work family. To keep the family functional, you must figure out how to get along with them all. Keep the relationships professional, but get to know everyone at least a little so you have formed some type of working relationship. Familiarizing yourself with everyone is necessary to avoid the negative aspects of office politics, determine networking and mentoring relationships, function successfully with the members of the group, and lead them when the opportunity presents itself.

Working toward mutually beneficial and satisfactory professional relationships with these various people is an ongoing act of mindfulness. Because the rest of them are not necessarily working toward that goal with the same care, strife is inevitable. Thus, you must be prepared to manage episodes of conflict with confidence and skill.

Conflict Management

Effective conflict management is a struggle for many people. Personalities are so varied that everyone tends to approach divergences differently. Without training in methods of conflict management, people resort to the manners most natural to the way they tend to handle things. Put two people in this sort of fight and you end up with one guy using his wrestling moves while the other is planting a karate chop. It may work in the ring, but it does not work in real-life conflict.

To handle conflict appropriately, those involved must adhere to a system of cooperation where the goal is to come to a solution. If one or both parties involved are not willing to work together or are more concerned with winning the fight rather than coming to a satisfactory conclusion to the discord, the conflict will not be managed successfully. Instead, the battle will continue with no true resolution. Multiple factors will influence whether conflict will be successfully managed.

Conflict management takes into account such aspects as the communication styles of both people involved, the perceptions held by each person about the other person, the shared history of both people involved, and the positions in the organization of the people involved. If you can understand and manage these aspects of the conflict, you can determine how best to solve the dispute.

Determining how another person is approaching the conflict will be much easier if you take into account how this person tends to communicate. Understanding this aspect will also illuminate why you and this person may have difficulty getting along, if that is the case. For example, if you are the type of person who always speaks your mind and this person keeps to himself, speaking up only when he gets angry, it is understandable how you two might end up butting heads. Take these differences into consideration and work forward from that vantage point. Recognizing the communication differences may be all it takes to manage the conflict.

Also to be considered is how much bad blood has already been built up thus far. If two people have a history of disagreement or have formed unbending biases against each other, conflict resolution will be difficult, because this may be their relationship. Sometimes people can get so caught up in the battle they may not even want to try to get along.

They resign themselves to disliking each other or, at times, may even simply come to enjoy the discord. In these types of cases, if conflict resolution is to be achieved, at least one of the fighting parties will need to reassess the relationship and come to the conclusion that it is a problem. Otherwise, there is no incentive to work on the relationship.

In some cases, the true problem between conflicting parties may be a battle of organizational positioning. For example, a subordinate who feels unjustified in his lower position may create subtle strife with the person above him he does not respect. Or, a person in a higher-level position may use that authority to attack a lower-level person whom she does not like. Sometimes these positional battles may take place between employees of the same level. If one person feels she is more qualified than a peer, for example, she may begrudge this person for being in the same organizational tier as she. This simple dynamic can be enough to create ongoing episodes of conflict.

Achieving collaboration in the process of conflict resolution is the goal, but, depending on those involved and the degree of conflict, a cooperative attempt at a solution may not be in the cards. However, if your ultimate goal is to work with the person to settle conflict, you must always be prepared to work with his or her particular communication and conflict resolution style. Consider the history and shared perceptions between you, your positions in the organization, and any other factor that you may believe is affecting your shared dynamic. Therefore, even as your conflict partner may avoid settling the dispute and carry on with your fight, your goal of unearthing an understanding of the conflict will still remain. Put aside those egotistical desires to be right or simply win, and work toward an honest resolution. Try enlisting the help of specific conflict resolution guidelines such as the "Conflict Management Checklist" by Cathie T. Siders and Carol A. Aschenbrener from the July-August, 1999 edition of the journal *Physician Executive©*. In some cases you may find you were the real problem all along. Although discovering your own blame in an episode of conflict can be humiliating, admit your fault and learn from the experience. Worse than becoming known as disagreeable in the office is becoming known as the too-prideful punk who never knows when to admit mistakes. Always be aware of the mistakes you may be making and be prepared to remedy the problems that have resulted.

The best way to avoid unnecessary and confusing conflict is simply to work toward getting along with the people whom you encounter at work. If you have functional, working relationships with the people in your office and the organization's network, you are more likely to have a peaceful existence in your workplace. Therefore, the first step toward carving your comfortable niche in the family is getting to know the people around you.

Know the People Around You

Knowing the people around you will help you to avoid negative conflict, but it can do even more for your career than just keep you in daily peacefulness. For example, some upper management types have been known to gauge an employee's character by how well he or she interacts with and treats others. Thus, maintaining at least a base level relationship with all those around you can help you in your climb up. Getting to know who is working around you can accentuate your interoffice growth in many other ways, too.

Knowing the people around you can provide many opportunities. Having a friend in the human resources department might give you an edge when an upper-level position opens up. That casual acquaintance in accounting might give you a leg up in figuring out a numbers query with minimal research. A payroll pal could provide you with the inside knowledge when someone is on the way out, leaving room for you on the way up. Workplace friends may help in getting you promoted, pick you to help them with a big project, assist in your transfer to their department, or even come in handy if they eventually leave your organization altogether. It pays to have friends in all places. Simply knowing who works in your office is a positive first step, but getting to know each one of them will benefit you even more. Begin building professional relationships with the people in your workplace, and you will see positive results in your daily experiences and your long-term career.

CASE STUDY: BRIAN ANTHONY

Brian Anthony

Mechanical Engineering Manager

Aerospace Industry

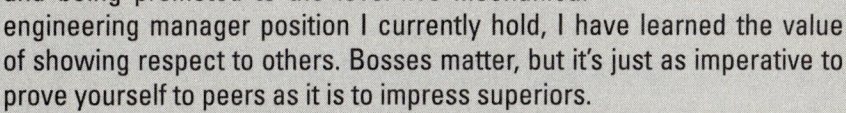

Through my years in the aerospace industry, starting out as an entry-level mechanical engineer and being promoted to the level-five mechanical engineering manager position I currently hold, I have learned the value of showing respect to others. Bosses matter, but it's just as imperative to prove yourself to peers as it is to impress superiors.

I have always liked to know what challenges my peers were facing so that I could figure out how I could make their jobs easier by doing my job better. At the end of the day, you need support from others to get your job done. Show respect for the people you work with, and they will help you achieve good things.

In my various positions, I have worked with individuals from all levels: subordinates, peers, senior managers, technicians, support personnel, and employees from many other disciplines. Each person takes a slightly different approach to the work. The better you are at reading different types of people and catering to how they each tick, the more successful you will be.

As you move up in an organization, you will appreciate having access to a greater network of people to help you continue to grow. It's all about building a strong network of relationships, so never burn a bridge. The professional world is way too small for that.

Building Relationships

A work family, much like your own relative clan, will most likely be plagued by episodes and instigators of dysfunction. Yet, these people who surround you are all members of the unit, so building relationships with them is essential. A perceived inability to play well with others will bode poorly to your character, while the perception that you have good relationships with others in the office will suggest that you have strong character. In addition to fostering positive perceptions, building good relationships will serve to help you learn and provide many advantages in the office.

Building a relationship in any realm is a continual work in progress. You cannot just plant the seed and expect it to grow. You must be willing to nurture your budding blooms with ongoing communication and concern or else, just like neglected sprouts, those relationships will wither and die. Expect to nurture your work relationships regularly so they keep growing, but do so as an ongoing experiment of enjoyment. Building relationships is meant to be fulfilling, after all.

Two major components of good relationship building are in the ability to develop respect for others and enact effective listening skills. Some work relationships you build will be made solely for the purpose of assembling satisfactory ties with all members of your work family. These relationships will be satisfying in some sense but not entirely fulfilling, as they may not flourish as some other relationships will. Still, you must continue to treat these individuals respectfully and use effective listening skills. Those relationships that begin to flow more naturally and effortlessly will also require that you continue to use these skills.

If you can assume the people with whom you interact have good intentions unless proven otherwise you will be able to develop a mutually beneficial feeling of respect for them. You can assume that you will not like every, most, or any aspects of other people's personalities, but you can be sure that each person deserves a fair chance at being treated with respect. Instead of focusing on those aspects of people that annoy you, try to focus on what you like, admire, or do not mind. It is much more pleasant to get along with people, and all that takes is treating them with the same respect you would want for yourself. Even in those relationships where you may occasionally question the respectability of others, your adherence to showing respect for even these types of people may assist in this person's dubious decorum and help you to maintain the high standards that will always make you look good. The other major component of good relationship building, practicing effective listening skills, will be equally advantageous to in your efforts.

Many people believe they are engaging in effective communication when, in actuality, they are missing out on the most vital aspect: listening. Being able to listen effectively will help you in all aspects of your life, not just relationship building. Effective listening occurs when you are able to successfully keep the lines of communication open, without monopolizing the dialogue, and can allow for and consider other people's points of view. Doing this will foster the building of honest relationships and help you to understand people. You could never understand them if you are missing out on what they have to contribute. These are the types of relationships through which you will learn and create new opportunities for yourself in the organization.

If you treat other people with respect and learn to listen to what they have to say, the result will be a legion of positive work relationships. This consequence will be of value, but you will be treated to another priceless reward, too: the honing of and greater potential for demonstration of your leadership skills.

When to Lead

Upper management is always on the lookout for a good leader. There are times, however, when seizing an opportunity to show your quality leadership skills can have a negative effect. Monopolizing, power-hungry show-offs are obnoxious in any setting. Why, then, would upper management choose to bring this sort of person up to their ranks? The answer, of course, is that they will not. Learning how to tell when it is a time to lead and when it is time to follow the leader is an essential component of being a promotable person.

Strong leadership is not about the ability to reign in the most power or exhibiting a strong, charming personality. These abilities may enable the possibility of leadership for some, but strong leadership skills are about possessing the ability to mobilize the troops. In the workplace, the troops are the throng of workers in your organization. Your ability to show leadership at work is contingent on your capacity to arouse cohesiveness, harmony, and collaborative efforts in the members of your organization and knowing when is the right time to lead. Some of the work is done when you build up your work relationships, but the rest of the work is done on the job: To be a successful leader you must be prepared to jump in and just do it.

If you are sincere in your efforts to be a positive leader, you have tackled half of the work of being one. Upper management will smell from a mile away a false attempt at stealing the leadership spotlight for the sake of brownie points. Thus, instead of focusing on simply appearing to be a leader, effectively work on learning positive leadership skills. For example, engaging in active listening — listening to and then repeating back the sentiments expressed by others — will give you the understanding you need to fully address issues of discussion. Additionally, you will show others that you value their opinions and take all angles into consideration. A good leader does not act unilaterally but directs the decision making to a unified experience. Ultimately, a good leader will then demonstrate the confidence and sense of responsibility needed to push the team toward a practical solution to any pressing quandary.

Networking

Working well with and learning to lead coworkers in your immediate office setting will be helpful in your career, but do not forget about those relationships in the broader network of your organization. This encompasses customers, clients, stockholders, those in related businesses, others in your field, and the working world at large. Anyone can be a potential component of your set of connections, so keep your eyes open to the possible networking opportunities.

Not all of us are social butterflies. Initiating conversations with others, even under the premise of making a work contact, can feel uncomfortable. But unlike approaching someone with whom you would like to strike up a friendly relationship, establishing a networking relationship is about creating a work-related, reciprocal tie. Professionally you have something to trade, such as resources or contacts.

Anywhere and everywhere are great places to network. If seeking networking opportunities, try an online portal that arranges networking events such as Netparty (**www.netparty.com**). Or, check out the local chapter of your profession's national organization with the Internet Public Library guide of associations (**www.ipl.org/div/aon**).

Successful networking can reap multiple rewards for you and your career. The main benefit of networking is, of course, that you will build up ties with people from whom you can learn. Every person has paved his or her own path through life, and so each person has at least something to offer in terms of what he or she has learned. Building contacts will help you to learn about new ideas and different perspectives, a boon to your understanding of your business and the world at large. Another powerful reason to build up your network is for the opportunities you might garner. Certainly, it is helpful to know people in high places, but sometimes it can be enough just to know people in various places. You never know where your connections might take you.

As you open yourself up to meeting new people, you may be lucky enough to find an individual who inspires you like no other. If you do, consider how this person might fit into your life as a mentor.

Mentors

Occasionally, you may discover the rare individual who inspires you to be a better person, try harder at work, and excel to the highest levels of your capacities. This gem is a mainstay of your network database and should be considered for mentorship potential. Everyone needs someone in his or her life to look up to and learn from. If you find someone like that, take advantage of the resource.

Throughout life you will encounter the occasional high-quality individual from whom you will take many lessons. Some of these individuals may become mentors in the most literal sense: guiding you, counseling you, and providing you lessons on life. Yet, your collective of mentors does not necessarily need to be part of a mutually acknowledged mentor-to-grasshopper relationship.

Your view of another person as someone from whom you can continuously learn may be all that takes place in the relationship. It may be that when you are in a difficult situation, you look to that person to determine how he or she might solve a particular conundrum This may be the extent of the relationship.

Other mentors in your life will play a more active role. You and a mentor may have the type of relationship in which you feel comfortable picking up the phone and getting his or her opinion on a problem you have at work. Perhaps you meet with this person regularly and discuss life, work, and each other's experiences. You may even form a relationship in which you can serve as mentor, too.

Whatever the nature of the relationship between you and your mentors, having people to whom you can look up and who contribute to your ability to make decisions, improve yourself, and solve problems will benefit your life. Keep yourself open to the idea of learning from others and finding the type of people who incite positive energy in you. Learning is a lifelong experience, and good teachers are everywhere.

You can do everything right in terms of cultivating positive work-related relationships and still find yourself in the middle of a mess with your coworkers. Consider the potentially negative effects of office politics.

Office Politics

When you open yourself up to relationships with your coworkers, you will inevitably encounter evidence of office politics. Although not all instances related to office politics are negative, the implication is that an element of misappropriated power will come into play. Your choice is whether to play the game and perhaps sell your soul in the process or opt out of the negativity associated with this dangerous game and risk ostracism, unknown penalties, and even sabotage.

In some workplaces, the culture of office politics can be so strong that all employees simply follow along, no questions asked, without even recognizing they are participating. For example, if the big boss in an organization tends to yell and treat subordinates poorly, this becomes a standard of treatment. Thus, every relationship in the organization may become laced with this sort of power dynamic. Certainly treating people this way is not right, and yet if it is an accepted component of office politics for the organization, the behavior becomes acceptable.

Ultimately, it is up to you to decide how you will behave at work. When faced with a choice between two unknowns, one laced with an element of dishonesty or negativity and the other an opportunity to demonstrate honor despite the potential for failure, the wise selection is to always go with honor. The draw of participating in office politics can be a sultry one, but no potential reward for dishonest or negative behavior should ever win out over the chance to show integrity.

Integrity is something that is often severely lacking in the workplace and when demonstrated does not always result in an obvious or immediately gratifying return. Yet, acting with integrity is one of the best career moves you will ever make.

Possible Pitfalls:

- Do not engage in petty office disagreements.

- Never miss an opportunity to diffuse a conflict appropriately.

- Do not belittle anyone whom you encounter on the job. Treat everyone, no matter how insignificant one may seem, with respect.

- Do not neglect your workplace relationships. Instead, nurture them on a regular basis (keeping in mind work productivity, of course).

- Avoid the negative aspects of office politics.

CHAPTER 11

Integrity

This week's checklist:

- Deconstruct your reputation in the office.

- Consider your personal rules for good customer service and apply them to how you treat those with whom you work.

- Determine what individual you trust most in your organization and figure out why.

- Ask a trusted friend how positive he or she perceives your character to be and why.

- Work on your ability to demonstrate dependability by noting how well you adhere to what you say you will get done and when.

Despite prevalence and perpetuation of the ongoing myth that all is fair in business, it turns out that you do not need to be a jerk to get ahead at work. Nice guys do not finish last.

Honesty, trustworthiness, kindness, dependability, loyalty, and sincerity are traits that will always serve you well in life and at work. Although it may be tempting to go to the dark side, it is not worth risking your karma for the slight possibility you may get ahead that way. Riding on the high road will always result in a smoother, more satisfying trip. Even if you do get ahead through wily, unseemly ways, the images you see of yourself in the mirror will remind you of the ugly acts you have committed in the name of furthering your career.

Instead, rise above those negative behaviors and, above all else, maintain your integrity and self-respect. Not only will you feel better about yourself, but other people will take notice, too, including upper-level professionals in your organization. "Do unto others as you would like others to do unto you" is not just a proverb. It is a way of life that will keep your integrity in check and allow you to look yourself in the mirror the next morning. Plus, it will serve to get you ahead at work.

When considering your integrity, there are a multitude of aspects to examine. Honesty is a vital component, and so too are dependability, loyalty, kindness, and sincerity. Each of these elements of integrity represents specific types of behaviors you can enact throughout your work day and that others will be able to recognize and name according to your actions. When your behaviors are laced with these virtuous characteristics, you will be confident in your integrity, and other people will begin to recognize you as a person who has integrity. However, some elements of integrity are not so clearly defined and depend on your willingness and ability to make virtuous choices.

Although being honest, dependable, kind, loyal, and sincere are fairly lucid aspects of integrity, other components are not so straightforward. Having good character, trustworthiness, and a positive reputation are also aspects of integrity. However, they are components that rely on one's ability to engage in a wide assortment of virtuous, though not as clearly defined, behaviors. Being loyal, for example, is contingent on your ability to consistently make appropriate choices. Ensure you are behaving with character and putting value in your good name and reputation.

With one week left before you go full gusto in your promotions negotiations, now is the best time to remember the value of your integrity. When faced with the possibility that others may need to be sold on your value, your integrity is the best insurance you have to preserve peace of mind.

When looking introspectively at how morally you have been conducting yourself in the workplace thus far, a simple spot to start is in considering your level of honesty. Throughout the course of any given day, you have multiple opportunities to either choose to be honest or dishonest, deceitful, even fraudulent in how you conduct yourself. Consider how you have been behaving.

CASE STUDY: MELISSA MERCHANT

Melissa Merchant

Retail Sales Manager

Alltel Communications, Inc.

I started out in my company as a customer service representative and have worked my way up through various leadership positions. My current position requires that I am responsible for seven different retail stores, and I have nine retail managers who report to me.

In my experience, the employees who get promotions are those who possess integrity, have an ability to inspire others, and who tend to serve the needs of others. Employees who demonstrate these characteristics tend to have successful leadership skills as well. They lead by example no matter if someone is watching or not and consistently choose the harder right versus the easier wrong. They recognize that leading people has to be about those who are following and not about acknowledging the skills of the leader. The rewards are in the accomplishments of those they serve, not in the efforts of the leader.

These types of employees succeed because they tend to treat everyone with the same sense of serving. They do not monopolize every opportunity for themselves. They point out contributions made by other individuals on the team. They are the go-to people who sacrifice themselves to help others succeed. In serving others' needs first, they become a significant person for professional and personal advice, in support of others' development, and in helping others to be better leaders and employees.

Honesty

Being honest with yourself can, at times, be even more difficult than maintaining honesty with others. A little white lie to your boss, "but I e-mailed that to you last week," to buy yourself more time to turn in an assignment today may never be discovered, but convincing yourself that you always do your best work when the devil on your shoulder insists otherwise is a harsh reality to escape in the long run. Your dishonesty will eventually catch up to your self-perception.

Let honesty prevail from the get-go. Your honest self should always keep a vigilant watch over all the choices you must make on a day-to-day basis. Even if you know you will get away with dishonest behaviors, choose now to be honest with yourself and others. At the end of the day, you have to live with yourself.

Throughout the course of every day, you have the choice of either being honest or being dishonest in the way you conduct yourself. Honesty and dishonesty can manifest in a number of ways, some of which you may not even consciously be aware. The most straightforward form of honesty is demonstrated through one's ability to tell the truth to the best of one's capacity. This, of course, can backfire and cause a negative result. If a person vows allegiance to the effort of being honest and thus hurts another person through a mean-spirited but honest comment, this negates the purpose of honesty. For example, if in the name of being honest, a person tells another person how ugly she thinks her new hairdo is, the result of so-called honesty becomes negative. Sometimes this type of honesty is necessary or expected, but it could serve to negate efforts to act with integrity if done with bad intentions. If someone manipulates the altruistic goal of acting with integrity to belittle others in the name of being honest, clearly he or she is not acting virtuously.

Being honest with integrity is not reliant on one's ability to tell the truth at all costs; it is about being honest with one's self and others for the purpose of acting with morality, for the sake of being a good person, and for adding to the positive nature of the world as opposed to robbing from it. For example, if you make a mistake and have the opportunity to cover your tracks and take it, you are not acting with honesty. If your boss asks you a question for which he earnestly wants your opinion and you choose to simply agree with his opinion in fear of experiencing negativity due to your disagreement, you are not acting with honesty. Your honesty can also be threatened through an act of omission. For example, if a person chooses to keep information inside as opposed to offering it to an individual who should rightfully have access to it, this person is demonstrating dishonesty.

To consciously choose honesty over dishonesty on a day-to-day basis, you must be prepared to thoughtfully mull over the opportunities presented to you. Sometimes dishonesty is merely a knee-jerk reflex resulting from the desire to pacify a situation rather than apply genuine care. That is, when one is presented with a choice of behavior, instead of considering what the right thing to do is, he or she instinctively responds in self-defense mode. In this way, the response is based more in a need to preserve oneself rather than act with integrity. For example, if a customer expresses dissatisfaction with a service you have provided and you recognize your responsibility for fault but choose to blame someone else, relying on your ability to smooth things over instead of being honest and admitting error, you have missed out on an opportunity to be honest.

As you go about your daily interactions, consider the opportunities presented to you. You will find multiple chances to be honest with yourself and others. If you have been living under the veil of knee-jerk responses, you may be surprised at how easy it can be to take the easy route and not worry about being honest. But if you pay attention, you will learn an important lesson: Being honest feels good to you, feels good to others, and will positively shape others' perceptions of you and your company.

One typical outcome of purposefully demonstrating honesty is the influx of trust others will place on you. People tend to trust people whom they typify as being honest. Although honesty is tied to trustworthiness, a number of other factors affect how well an individual is trusted.

Trust

Trustworthiness in the workplace is on the downswing, according to a recent workplace survey conducted by Paul Bernthal, Senior Research Consultant for Development Dimensions International a workforce strategies firm. Roughly half of respondents claimed distrust in their workplace organizations and the people within. Some of the most oft-cited behaviors that bred this distrust were tendencies toward protecting one's welfare over all else and avoidance of taking responsibility for personal mistakes in lieu of placing outward blame. Clearly, people who think only of themselves and cannot admit their mistakes are pegged as untrustworthy.

It is a shame that the virtue of trust appears to be so lacking in the workplace environment these days, because trust is such a vital ingredient to cohesive teamwork. Employees and employers are less able to rely on each other and work in cooperation. Although the would-you-catch-me-if-I-fell-back scenario has been beaten to a pulp through its abundant use at every team-building workshop since the 1980s, it still remains a tried-and-true analogy. Ask yourself whether you are the type of person others in your workplace would trust to catch them. If you are not, it is a lot to expect that you can trust each other to work in tandem.

To trust each other, organizational members must be able to rely on each other's words, behaviors, and intent. When an individual has proven to misrepresent him or herself in any of these areas, the trustworthiness of this individual becomes questionable. If, however, an individual can consistently demonstrate that what he or she says and does can be trusted and that his or her tendency is to act in goodwill toward fellow organizational members, this person will be deemed trustworthy.

To develop your genuine trustworthiness, you must build a pattern of trustworthy behavior. To do this, you must strive to be honest in your words and behaviors and do so in goodwill for others. This goes back to what was said before about using honesty with the goal of altruism, as opposed to using honesty as an absentminded weapon against being perceived as being dishonest or using honesty as an excuse to say whatever you want to whomever you want. If you continuously work toward communicating with others honestly and with good intentions, taking other people's feelings under consideration, and being open to admitting mistakes, you will soon be perceived as a trustworthy individual.

Honesty and trustworthiness are essential hallmarks of integrity, but so too is the ability to treat others with kindness. Although a business's customers are just one grouping of people to learn to treat well, the philosophy of good customer service is a model to follow when attempting to treat others in your workplace and those with whom you come in contact with in your work life with kindness.

Customer Service

The idea of good customer service, as used in this section, is not used solely in reference to any literal customers but as an allusion to a positive customer service philosophy: Treat everyone you encounter on the job with the kindness expected in good customer service. In this sense, your customer service skills may be applied to stockholders, coworkers, couriers, waiters, computer technicians, and more. Consider these basic rules of good customer service: Provide quality service that exceeds expectations, attempt to avoid arguments and opt for courtesy instead, and assume the best of other people unless given hard evidence to the contrary.

The first rule of good customer service is in assurance that you are supplying quality service, products, and behaviors that exceed expectations. In every one of your interactions you should attempt to treat people with the kindness they deserve and then some. One tactic top managers use to identify workers who may be lacking in integrity is to observe how they treat the people who seemingly have no effect on their careers. For example, if an individual treats upper management professionals with kindness but balks rudely at the busboy's mistakes, clearly this person is more concerned with appearing kind rather than being kind. Unless you have been given clear indication otherwise, you should anticipate that the people you encounter will appreciate engaging in positive communication with you. Approach them in this regard, and your interactions will be fruitful and positive.

The second rule of good customer service is to avoid arguments and strive to apply courtesy, instead. For a variety of reasons, the occasional person with whom you must interact on the job might incite an argument with you. Perhaps you may have played a role in the initiation of this potential fight, or maybe the combatant simply woke up tired, missed his bus, or is having a bad case of "the Mondays." Whatever the reason and whether the fault is yours, do not get caught up in a workplace brawl or any sort of rambunctious altercation that could jeopardize your attempts to act with integrity. If someone tries to get you involved in an argument, maintain your composure and engage with him or her as courteously as you can. Apologize for any wrongdoing on your part and apply your conflict management skills, attempting to calm the situation and strive to come to a solution rather than be victorious in the argument. You do not want to become known for being argumentative, even if you did not start the fight and you know you are right. Settle your conflicts professionally, courteously, and calmly.

The third rule of good customer service is in assumption of other people's good intentions. If you can always assume that other people are behaving with positive intentions, it will help you to stay true to the goal of remaining kind in all of your interactions. When someone approaches you with a lilt to his or her voice that you interpret as being mean-spirited, take a step back and reconsider your reactions. You cannot fully comprehend why this person would be mean to you or if that is this person's intention. Simply, keep to your efforts of practicing kindness to the best of your capabilities. In the real world, not everyone is going to be nice and act with good intentions, but the bad behavior of other people does not serve as any cause for you to be swayed to act inappropriately. Civility should be your standard and, if other people would prefer to be mean and yell and treat people poorly, always know that is their problem and not yours. You do not have to put up with it, and you certainly do not need to engage in it.

Another vital aspect to consider is your dependability. The virtue of being dependable is another essential aspect of your moral strength.

Dependability

Being a dependable person is something that will help you find success in all aspects of your life. Just as you appreciate the people in your life who you can depend on, you want people to expect the same good results from you as well. The only way to encourage others to believe you are a dependable person is to behave accordingly. To be dependable, you should strive to be someone other people can count on in a crisis, do what needs to be done on a regular basis, and always stay true to your word.

Occasionally, a workplace crisis will crop up that needs immediate attention. Although you cannot be expected to successfully put out the fire every time, you should be willing to step up and offer, brainstorm, or apply a solution to the problem as often as possible. Cowering in the corner because you do not want to put yourself on the line of responsibility or because you are entrenched in some other project does not present you well. To be dependable, other people should be able to anticipate your willingness to care about solving office problems. If you are always willing to help, this demonstrates you care about the organization and can be counted on to help the people involved in the organization.

On a regular basis you are presented with opportunities to demonstrate that you can be depended on to do work for the good of the organization and the people involved in it. For example, adhering to the established deadlines of your projects will demonstrate to the people in your organization that you value the importance of keeping the machine running properly. After all, if you choose to ignore your responsibilities, other people in the organization may not be able to tend to their responsibilities. You have a responsibility to keep up with the demands of your job. If you cannot be depended upon to do so, the efficiency of the organization is jeopardized, other people in the organization may be affected, and the office culture of dependability is compromised.

Arguably, the most important aspect of dependability is having the ability to stay true to your word. If you do not make the effort to take part in tending to crisis situations, this can be forgiven. If you occasionally deviate from dependably tending to the details of your job, this too can be forgiven. But if you demonstrate that you cannot stay true to your word, you will swiftly earn the reputation of being undependable. If you say you are going to do something, then do it. If you are skeptical about whether you can complete something that needs to get done, do not say that you will do it.

Every day you have opportunities to showcase your dependability. When given the opening to show your dependable nature, by all means do so. Conversely, if you simply cannot do what needs to get done, you will do yourself the worst disservice if you say you will do it but do not follow through. For example, if you tell your boss that you will complete an assignment but do not turn it in on time or do not do the job professionally and according to specifications, you are showing that you are not dependable. But if you stay true to your word, do what your job entails on a regular basis, and are ever ready to help create solutions for office problems, you will earn a good reputation. People who are perceived as being dependable are one of the best types of people to have in any office setting, and being able to effectively cultivate this tendency will be a boon to your promotable appeal.

In addition to the components of integrity examined so far, loyalty is another vital component of having **integrity**. Loyalty can be expressed in numerous ways and for different people but is always a valuable trait to possess.

Loyalty

Loyalty is a trait that is vital in quality employees. In this current culture of entitled thinking, it is easy to get sucked into despair when things do not seem to be going your way at work. Instead of sticking with the company, employees become convinced that another organization may have greener grass and, of course, more cash.

Employers and managers know that this temptation is a fact of the marketplace and often implement incentives into their system to boost employee retention and satisfaction. This is all well and good, especially when you are the recipient of a bonus, valuable gift, or are treated to a company leisure retreat. However, this type of system contingent on rewards (or bribery, depending on how it is enacted or perceived) does not breed loyalty. An organization that leans on this type of system to encourage employee retention may likely find that, if the gravy train stops pouring or the employees become displeased with the gravy, their employees are not loyal. What appeared to be loyalty was gratitude, at first, and then entitlement next.

Bonuses, gifts, and other incentives are certainly nice things for your boss to offer, but do not come to expect them, grow dependant on them, or, worst of all, become disgruntled when something changes in the system of using them. You agreed to the job you have under the condition that X was your salary. Sure it is nice to receive additional benefits, but X is the amount you assumed would take care of your expenses. Even if a trend has been set in which you occasionally receive more cream off the top, be happy for the skim milk you get until you put yourself in the promoted position to accept more.

Our culture of materialism is extraordinarily high at this point in time. As a result of or, at least, in relation to this dependency on owning a vast and impressive army of consumer goods, people often find their unnecessary desires confused with their actual needs. But it is rare that we need those things we desire: a better car, a bigger house, and designer clothes. Loyalty is an admirable quality that should not be linked to how well our employee leads us to better material goods. Maybe it feels like jobs are a dime a dozen, but you would be surprised at how many poorly run organizations there are out there. If you are content with your bosses, the organization, and your job at large, be grateful that you have found a good situation, and reward them with your loyalty.

In this discussion on acting with integrity, the idea of honesty was covered. Sincerity also warrants coverage. Honesty is linked to sincerity, but possessing the ability to be sincere is an altogether different concept.

Sincerity

Asking some people to be sincere is like asking them to lick their own tongue. Requesting sincerity from an insincere person is an impossible demand and one unlikely to facilitate a genuine response. But if you have a desire to be more sincere or, at least, want to learn how to coax out that side of you, you can achieve that goal.

Confucius once said, "Sincerity and truth are the basis of every virtue." I hope this philosophy has been stressed throughout this book. Although you have been urged to try different things and explore new ways to express yourself, do not confuse this with being untrue to your genuine self. The basis for living well, like Confucius suggested, is found through sincerity. How then, in this world where fake seems so dominant and is often rewarded, can you tap into being sincere?

At times, you act stronger than you feel. We revert to "knowing it all" to shield from others how much we believe we do not know. Sometimes we even do seemingly good things, like put on the world's biggest phony smile or offer to do something kind for someone else to appear sweet, just to hide the devil that lurks inside. Sure, it is still good to do nice things even when our motivation is all out of whack, but what about getting in the habit of doing nice things just because the world is better place when people are nice to each other?

The No. 1 rule of sincerity is being true to what you honestly feel in your heart, so what if the truth is that you honestly do not have good feelings emanating from your heart? I hope that is not the case and, somewhere in there, you are hopeful of mankind, genuinely care about others, and can feel compassion on another's behalf. But let us say you are not. Let us say that, for reasons of childhood trauma, lifetime experiences, or even just the feeling you get about people through no actual bad experiences that tarnished your views, you just do not have much love for people. If this is your sincere standpoint, it is a part of who you are, so just go with it. Do not be afraid to live your life wary of others in this world, but be honest that this is how you feel. To pretend otherwise and to present yourself as a jolly soul who has love for everyone would be insincere. Maybe, though, you will be able to start seeing what is good in this world and reconsider your point of view.

Regardless, we all have horrible thoughts from time to time. Some of us may have more horrible thoughts than good. Being your most sincere self is about being open and allowing yourself to be the you that you are behind closed doors, flaws and all. Sincerity is not something that can be easily faked. People will see through that charade. So if you are simply playing the part of the outgoing guy, the smart girl, or the kindhearted do-gooder when, in actuality, you do not always feel like being on stage, you question your intelligence, or you do not always feel like being so nice, look inside yourself and see where the true you is in all of that. You are likely not fooling anyone but yourself anyway.

Beware, however, that if you do let it all hang out, you are leaving yourself open to a new scrutiny. Not everyone will like the real you. When people have a problem with the fake you, the pain is not so harsh. After all, it was just an act anyway. But if you allow this sincere, honest version of you to be seen, then you are welcoming judgment. Bad reviews may be painful, but in the long run you will see the benefits of being your most sincere self. Why go through life just pretending to be a good person? Be your sincere self and hone the good person inside of you.

The components to integrity that have been examined thus far may contribute to your character. However, the idea of having good character is contingent on many other additives, as well.

Character

Think about what it means to have character. You may be able to name a few people in your life whom you would deem as having good character. It is not something you are necessarily born with but rather something that becomes fine-tuned through the course of your life. Having good character is tied in with the tune of your attempts at demonstrating personal integrity, but it is more specific to how your choices in life stack up in the long run to reveal your truly positive nature.

When faced with a choice between right and wrong, do you tend to do the right thing even if the consequence to yourself might not be most beneficial? Is this how others would perceive your typical series of actions? To build the reputation of having a good character, you need to be prepared to demonstrate your attuned ability to weed out wrong choices from your selection of the right ones. It is one thing to know what you should do, but it is another to consistently show that you will make the right choices no matter the possible negative results to yourself.

Having good character encompasses all the aspects of demonstrating integrity, but there is a subtle difference between the two. Although integrity is about being able to adhere to a code of ethical rules, having good character is a part of you. If a person has a positive character, he or she will intrinsically make the right decisions in life. In some cases, an individual is simply born with these good-natured tendencies. In other cases, an individual will so effectively learn the important lessons in life that he or she will adopt the morality of those lessons and apply them without even having to think about right and wrong.

A potential result of building good character, and all efforts pertaining to improving one's integrity, is a positive reputation.

Reputation

Keeping a good reputation is much easier than washing away a bad one. If you have been attuned all along to the value of maintaining your integrity, your reputation should already be tip-top. If you have engaged in any shady practices, participated in interoffice gossip sessions, or conducted yourself in such a way as to discredit your reputation, you have some work to do.

First impressions stick fast and hard, so you may not be able to rectify your reputation according to some people. Until you part, these people may stick with their initial assumptions about your character, whether their assessments are based in reality or not. For those more flexible creatures, if you have earned yourself any bad marks on your reputation scorecard, all you can do is begin cleaning up that mess and hope for the best. If you are guilty of gossip, for example, stop that bad habit immediately. Gossip participation only shows through your insecurities and the desire to elevate yourself above those whom you are talking about. Even gossiping about celebrities can shine a negative light on your character. Think of more valuable things to discuss. Who cares if Debbie in accounting is canoodling with Tom in human resources or that Brad Pitt and Angelina Jolie are adopting another baby? Focus on what matters or is applicable to advancing your knowledge and place at work and in life.

You want to have a reputation that speaks highly of you, not one that makes people question your values, work ethic, and integrity. Some people involved in your rise up may not even have the opportunity to spend time with you one on one, so why give them ammunition to assess you poorly without having even met you? If you did not tend to your good name from the get-go, start acting with good character now so your reputation may have a chance at rectification.

You should feel positive about yourself if you have taken steps toward ensuring your integrity is intact. The other lessons in these past weeks have maybe given you a sense of confidence as well. You should see that you have much to offer and feel eager to apply what you have learned in this process. With this newfound positivity, confidence, and plan of attack, you are almost ready to go. However, you need a few more bits of encouragement to prepare yourself for the upcoming promotion discussions. In the next section we will examine a few important points of how to prepare for the big day.

Possible Pitfalls:

- Resist the urge to tell someone your true but hurtful feelings in the name of honesty.

- Become the type of person others can trust.

- Treat all people with appropriate levels of respect.

- Hone your character by engaging in virtuous behaviors.

- Avoid assuming that the grass is greener in other organizations and work toward becoming a loyal employee in your organization.

CHAPTER 12

The Big Day!

This week's checklist:

- Practice, practice, practice.

- Over-prepare for all possibilities.

- Put together the items of clothing that will give you a confident boost in your meeting.

- Ask a trusted friend to stage a mock meeting with you.

- Practice any strategies you may enlist to calm yourself down during low lights of the meeting.

You have put in the hard work. You have done your research, refined yourself, and have the confidence to present yourself well on the big day. Do not run out the door just yet. This week you will be presenting your boss with your official plan to move yourself up in the organization. Although you have the supporting data to show you are ready to rise, you, the package itself, need to support your claim as well.

Your appearance, communication, and the presentation need to be impeccable. After all the work you have put in to lead up to this day, you do not want to miss an opportunity due to a mere technicality. You must look the part so that your boss can picture you in the new position. You should be well rehearsed in conveying the important points to your boss so there is no confusing what you are expecting. You must feel confident and comfortable in your role so that you, the product, are presented in its best light. All along in this process you have assessed and corrected any standout complications in your presentation. Now you will put these lessons to play in one showcase of what you have learned.

To ensure your presentation plays out according to your well-planned designs, you must put in some work beforehand to prepare fully for any potential roadblocks. This week is your last opportunity to do the preparation work. Do not leave anything to chance. Over-prepare if you must, but make sure you come to the meeting fully prepared to make your requests and back it all up.

Being prepared with the information is one aspect, but equally important is being well rehearsed. You do not want to come into the meeting expecting to give a monologue and be thrown off because your boss keeps interrupting. Instead, practice in a variety of ways to cover all potential deviations from the meeting you imagined.

One potential scenario may arise in management of the flow of conversation. In a situation such as this, where you are put face to face with a person whom you may not talk to so openly or about an issue that is so highly important and personal to you, a potential outcome may be stage fright. This can manifest in multiple ways, but the most devastating outcome for you could be that the lines of communication could become muddled with the tension. Therefore, you must guard your investment in time, energy, and hopes for your future by ensuring you keep the flow of productive communication going by any means possible.

With everything that has gone into this big day and the potential for what could result from it, you may find yourself losing your cool. Protect yourself ahead of time by coming up with tactics to ward off any negative feelings that might crop up during the process if you begin to feel frustrated or nervous. You may already have some techniques that you use to diffuse situations where you start to feel your temper rise, but if not, this chapter will cover one popular method for immediate stress relief that could work for you.

Another important aspect to prepare for involves the manner in which you will physically present yourself. Appearances do matter. In this solitary time capsule of how your boss will perceive you, your appearance will matter all the more. You have an opportunity to present yourself exactly as you would like your boss to see you. Take the time to make the physical package appear put together, and your boss will be more likely to believe that you are just that.

There are plenty of things to consider before you head into your meeting, but the first step should be in getting everything together in preparation of the big day.

Preparation

In these past three months you have put in the work to make these few days before the meeting go as easily as possible. There is no sense in cramming now. Have confidence in yourself and the in-depth, introspective process through which you have put yourself. Take this time before you present your case at the meeting to revel and relax: Revel in all that you now know about yourself, and relax with the confidence that comes from being prepared to take on a challenge.

Picture yourself in the meeting: discussing with your boss what you hope to gain and how you are prepared for it, exchanging an appropriate dose of pleasant banter, and feeling confident because you have a good defense for your case. Your boss's response should be in direct correlation to the reasonableness of your request and how well you will present it.

As if you are packing for a trip, gather up the tangible items you will be bringing in to the meeting. Compile the printed materials you will be bringing to the meeting, either for your own consultation or to provide to your boss, and put them in the order in which you will likely bring them into play. Familiarize yourself with them again so you are prepared to use them appropriately, comfortably, and not as though you are reading a shopping list to your boss. Along with the printed materials, collect any other items you envision needing for the meeting: your favorite coffee mug, a lucky rabbit's foot, and others.

After you have physically and mentally compiled every item that you want presented in your case for a promotion, you will want to put it all together in a mock practice for the meeting.

Practice

In this context, practice for the big day is not about perfecting your presentation, making sure you know what you will be talking about, or even coming up with a killer anecdote to win your boss over. Practice, in this sense, is all about gauging how the process will feel. Through this you will see that this meeting, just like any other event, is not that big of a deal. It is an exchange of ideas just like any other work meeting, and, although the meeting is all about you, you certainly have a right to your opinion. You fully believe you are ready for this next step in your career, and this is your chance to convince your boss that your opinion is right.

You could easily conduct this practice meeting with your reflection in the mirror but, better yet, ask a trusted friend to engage in a mock exchange with you. If you have checked with human resources, your employee handbook, or a coworker who has gone through the process to learn details of the procedure of promotion negotiations, you should have a good sense of how the process plays out. If you have a more ambiguous idea of the procedures, as would be the case if you do not know anyone who has gone through it or there are no set rules for the process, leave it to your imagination. Play out the possible scenes as you imagine they might pan out. Likely, you will hit on something close to the truth, but certainly you will gain some confidence in how well you will be able to manage the process when the time comes.

If you conduct your practice with a friend who already has a good idea of your work life, still take a few minutes to explain who you are at work, what your boss is like, and what the possible roadblocks in the path toward your promotion will be. Then, set up the scenario just as though you anticipate the actual event will occur: seating arrangement, coffee cup on the table, and paperwork in your briefcase. Just like in the real event, you may be responsible for leading the flow of the discussions, so take advantage of this opportunity to encourage the presentation to run its course exactly as you envision it. Enjoy this practice: Talk about your successes, what your goals are for the organization, and why you are ready for a promotion.

As you practice, take some time to consider the application of your conversational skills. You may think you should practice as though you will be controlling all aspects of the communication, but your boss could engage you in a simple conversation instead.

Conversation

Practicing your presentation in the realm of a mock meeting should have shown you how easy it can be to talk about what you want. But translating that feeling to the actual meeting is easier said than done for individuals who get stage fright, have low self esteem, or have a difficult time with their social or communication skills. These types of hindrances can keep people back their whole lives, and so to suggest that we examine ways around them is too simplistic. If you are an individual who suffers from any affliction that makes the prospect of this meeting feel like a walk on a plank, there is no definite answer to your dilemma that can be applied here in the short term. However, it can be worthwhile to anyone, not just this anxious population, to keep a few usable techniques in a corner of your mind that may help if you find yourself tongue-tied, nervous, or feeling as if you are not communicating your case well.

One easy technique involves planting an idea in your subconscious to be accessed if some anxiety starts creeping into the conversation. Often the problem is simple mind over matter. Being in a situation in which you are being judged is hard for anyone. Feeling inferior as a result of being judged may trigger a typical tendency toward a demonstration of hampered social skills. Experts suggest that, in preparation for such an event, you have at the ready a self-appreciating mantra or image to ward off those negative feelings and resulting decline in communication skills. Remember Stuart Smalley? He may be just a silly SNL character, but his method may work for you. Everyone, at some time or another, feels as if he or she is not good enough. Block that sentiment from tainting your esteem and conversation skills by replacing it with words of personal encouragement.

Keep the conversation light but on track. Your and your boss's time is precious. You have scheduled this meeting to discuss the specific matter of your promotion. Your positive attitude and likability may affect the result so you do not want to miss that opportunity to sway, but keep the flow of the discussion on the matter at hand. You have points to make and evidence to support your claim, so it is up to you to communicate that.

At some point during the process, you may find yourself questioning your success in the meeting or how your boss might be receiving what you have to say. Do not let the fear of failure get you down. Maintain your cool temperament.

Keeping Your Cool

Week 5 examined a vital component to getting organized: the ability to de-stress yourself. In that context, the idea was to add pleasant activities or routines to your life to avoid stress overload. In the context of maintaining your cool at the meeting, your personal de-stress tricks may be all you need. If you like to calm down with a soothing cup of tea, for instance, there may be a place for that in the meeting. If you like to do step aerobics to de-stress, you may want to pick up a new trick.

Rage is a common reaction to everything these days. Bad driving, a bad grade, and poor service, for example, may be all it takes to get someone going. Keeping your cool is beneficial to all involved. The benefits for you are keeping your blood pressure down and not looking like a fool. The benefit for the person who gets the brunt of your rage is avoiding the wrath of your pent-up hostility. Simply counting from one to five or taking a deep breath may be all you need to curb the unnecessary drama of rage unchecked. Even if the person who is involved in your anger deserves a tongue lashing, it is always better for you to keep your cool.

Plenty of triggers could throw off your game, so simply do not let them. Have a plan ready in case you find yourself getting anxious or angry. For example, implement deep breathing exercises to reduce the tension or try visualization methods to calm yourself down. Practice these techniques beforehand so you can gauge their potential for successfully diffusing a bad reaction on your part. Nothing will kill your chances faster than being perceived as a hothead who cannot take the slightest hint of criticism. Stay calm and respond clearly to any potential disagreement your boss may have with your presentation. You have already prepared for such an instance when you came up with your preemptive counterarguments, after all.

Being able to stay professional and calm in the heat of any discord thrown your way will bode well for your presentation, but take care of those first impressions, too. Make sure you come to the meeting pressed and dressed to impress.

Appearance

Week 6 examined briefly how usual it is for others to judge us by our appearance. Cleanliness presents you well, and dressing your façade up with appropriate apparel is important in communicating a positive message about who you are as a person and employee. You should be taking time each day to present yourself as a person who cares about sending that positive message but, especially on this important day, you want to impress upon your boss that you care so much about this opportunity that you have dressed even better for the special occasion. In addition to sending your boss a positive message, you will boost your own confidence, because presenting yourself positively on the outside easily breeds feeling positive on the inside. Give yourself that extra boost by putting on your most powerful ensemble and start the day knowing that you have, at least, presented your outside package as best you can. Starting with that confidence will lend to the evolution of a day that starts good and gets only better.

In preparing for the big day, plan exactly what you will wear and have it ready to go ahead of time (ironed and accessorized) to eliminate any unnecessary stress on the day of your meeting. If you have not worn the exact combination of clothing before, try it on to ensure it still fits appropriately, conveys the message you are intending to send, and goes together as a complete outfit. Take into account the other controllable aspects of your physical appearance as well. For instance, if you have a piercing that is ordinarily acceptable in the office or a pronounced badge of facial hair, consider how those adornments will affect the perceptions of your boss. The meeting is essentially a job interview; you are trying to procure a new position, so follow a few rules relevant to putting together an interview look that will work for you.

Dress for success:

- If you can wear it out to a club, it is not appropriate garb for this meeting or, likely, the office.

- Wear something comfortable, both in fit and how you feel about yourself in it. If something binds your movement, causes you to fiddle with it, or leaves you questioning how good you look, reconsider your choice.

- Unless you are in a creative industry such as fashion, conservative and overdressed is preferable to casual or underdressed.

- Shoes say a lot about a person. Scuffed and overused shoes may give off the impression that you do not pay attention to details. A clean, well-kept pair will convey a sense of pleasant precision.

- Although stylized trim such as tattoos, piercings, distinctively different hairstyles, and facial hair are commonplace, the truth is that many people will still judge an individual based on these types of ornamentation. If you feel it could sidetrack from your potential in the workplace and you are comfortable downplaying, changing, or hiding these elements of your look, consider that option.

- In lieu of heavy perfumes or aftershave lotions, stick with a nice cleansing shower or bath the morning of the meeting. Being confined in a small space with a walking bottle of product can be distracting and asphyxiating.

- Stick with safe color, style, and fabric options. A dark, traditional two-piece natural-fiber suit is a safe bet for both women and men. Interesting colors, styles and patterns are ever changing and dependent on personal preferences. You do not want your clothes to be what your boss notices first, so it is best to stick with a conservative yet attractive look over an outfit that will take center stage over your presentation.

- Grooming accents such as nails, cosmetics, and body hair should appear polished and well maintained. Excessive makeup, scraggly nails, or wild facial, head, or other hair will convey the wrong message. Keep these styling accents to a conservative minimum.

- Purses, portfolios, and briefcases can provide polish to a look and serve to transport your substantiating materials. If you do bring in such an item, please ensure that it is clean, in good repair, and will not distract from your professional appearance (for example, a bag with a silly slogan, your college backpack, or the dinosaur of a briefcase your dad handed down to you).

- Most important, consider your field, organization, potential position, and the person with whom you will be having the meeting when considering the physical appearance you are creating.

How you present yourself in this meeting will affect the outcome of your promotion-related requests. But it is not the minor communication gaffes, ill-conceived clothing color scheme, or split-second loss of cool that will hurt you. Poor choices and nervous stumblings are human. Minor sprinklings of imperfections are inevitable. Do not let these difficulties distract you from all that you have accomplished at work, your efforts at following through in this promotion plan, and the overriding goal of growth in your professional life. You are prepared for this meeting and have every right to ask for the opportunity to move up. Do not let a stumbling block or two hold you back from getting what you want.

You are now ready to go get that promotion. But before you forge ahead, you may want to look at the next section, Chapter 13. In it you will learn the top reasons why promotions are denied. Some reasons may give you ideas as to what you should make sure to do or not do at the meeting. Others may provide some insight into those uncontrollable reasons why you may not get the promotion you desire. Either way, you will be better prepared to head into the meeting knowing full well what you are up against.

Possible Pitfalls:

- Do not underdress for the occasion.

- Do not miss anything that could hold you back. Examine all angles.

- Avoid appearing underprepared: practice, practice, practice.

- Do not get caught up in the points of your presentation. Remember to learn from the experience.

- Avoid losing your cool.

CHAPTER 13

Top Ten Reasons Promotions Are Denied

The road to success is not paved with the most consistently good attempts at moving up, just the most consistent number of attempts at moving up. Thus, the more often you put yourself out there and make genuine efforts to get your career going, the more likely you will be to make strides closer to the goal of moving up in your organization. It is a simple matter of percentages.

Assume you will find success on 5 percent of the occasions in which you make attempts to contribute to the goal of moving up in your organization. For the sake of this example, let us say that "success" is defined as effectively leaving the impression on your boss that you are a valuable employee and someone to watch for potential upward mobility. If you were to make 20 attempts this year to advance at work, you would likely prove successful just one time. That is, your boss would consciously note one time this year that you are special, and the rest of the time you will sort of fade back into the background with the rest of the employees who are just getting by. However, if you go into work every day, do your best work, exceed the demands of the job, and mindfully make consistent attempts to do something extraordinary at work, you will create more occasions in which to get ahead. Each day, if you make just two conscious attempts at doing something special for the organization, trying out a new idea, or seizing a growth opportunity, by the end of the year you will succeed at getting your boss's attention about 25 times. This kind of consistency will rack up and leave the notion with your boss that there is something extra special about you.

Those successful in business are not so simply because they have always been right, are necessarily smarter than you, or have successful outcomes every time they attempt to succeed. They have kicked and scratched their way to the top, not accepted defeat, are always trying to find ways to meet success, and consistently learn from their so-called failures. They are not afraid of failure, and they embrace opportunities created through failures just as much as they do the opportunities resulting in successes.

In reality, successful people rack up more failures than the apparent failures of the business world. Successful people simply try more times and, thus, fail more times, but they

CHAPTER 13: TOP TEN REASONS PROMOTIONS ARE DENIED

learn from their mistakes and just keep trying. In their grand amassment of failed attempts lies the successes that have gotten them where they are.

Think of it like the world's casino: the more quarters you put in, the more likely you are to succeed. But it is even better than that because every quarter you put in builds on the last one (unlike playing the slots in Vegas). Every time you try, you have a chance to win. So what if you do not win every time? You learn through those experiences and up your chance for success the next time by applying those lessons the next round. You may end up investing 100 quarters (a hundred attempts at success), but you have 100 times greater chance at winning than if you had not invested a single quarter.

Of course, in your attempts at success, you will be faced with a countless array of roadblocks. Life does not just hand you what you want, after all. The fruits of your labor will taste sweeter when you work for them, though. Some of these barriers will be in your control, and some will be completely uncontrollable. That means there is a chance that you will do everything you should be doing and still not get what you want or even deserve. Certainly, the more you try the more chances you will have to succeed, but sometimes you cannot control the outcome, no matter how hard you try to succeed and no matter that you technically did everything right.

Consider your efforts in this process toward getting the promotion you want. You can make exponential strides in all areas of your work existence and still not find the success you crave, are prepared for, and deserve. You can make exponential strides in all areas of your work existence and still not find the success you crave, are prepared for, and deserve. To help you determine what further steps you should take to prevent denial of your promotion, consider the top ten categories of reasons promotions are typically rejected.

Interference with Prescribed Hierarchical Protocol

Workplace hierarchy structures are determined through the rationale of past and present organization participants, workforce and specific industry trends, and hierarchical protocols. Some organizations will be inflexible in their interpretation of these spoken and unspoken rules. Top managers claim that it is due to adherence to a prescribed hierarchical protocol that interferes with many promotion requests. Pay scales and position changes are often considered on a schedule or productivity scale. Individuals who are unaware of the protocol or believe that their performance supersedes the way things are done may find disappointment.

Bottom line: Find out if your organization has an official or unofficial hierarchical protocol. If your promotion request is not in line with company standards, do not sweat it too much. You got the meeting with your boss, so threat of failure or not, he or she is willing to consider your appeal.

No Money in the Budget

Top managers cite the reason of having no money in the budget for promotion-related raises even as anecdotal evidence suggests that this rationale for promotion denial can be a shifty one. Clearly, there are many instances in which organizations will simply not have the financial resources for promotion-associated pay increases. However, according to top managers, the "no money in the budget" justification is often used as an easy excuse because the organizational heads determine that the promotion applicant is not ready for the next level, the employee will remain loyal with or without the raise, or the employee will be willing to take on more responsibilities first and then be rewarded with a pay raise later.

Bottom line: Consider the financial state of your organization and the economy if you are requesting a specific pay raise in association with your promotion. If you have access to the specifics of the organizational budget or know of appropriate corners that could be cut to allow for your raise, keep that knowledge at hand as you attend your meeting. If the "no money in the budget" rationale is thrown your way, that does not have to mean an end to negotiations. Stick with your nonmonetary promotion requests and work toward a specific pay raise clause to apply in your near future. Your employers will be impressed that your goal is to grow in the organization even without immediate financial gain.

Hassle of Staff Changes

Consider this possible scenario: Employee A moves to a higher position. As a result, the employer moves Employee B out of her present position to fill the abandoned slot of Employee A. Then, the employer moves Employee C from his position to fill Employee B's discarded post. Based on this type of interoffice shifting, a seismic quake of employee movement can result. And that does not even take into account the outward venturing the employer may have to embark on to fill the empty positions with the best possible candidates.

Bottom line: Keep an ear out for higher-level openings. If you can anticipate the opportunity before your employers spend resources filling the position, you have saved them money, time, and energy they would have otherwise spent on seeking out the right person. Then, to make things easier in the filling of your position, find the person in your office who is most likely to be an appropriate replacement for you and groom him or her for the job. Also, ensure that the transition into your role will be smooth by keeping everything associated with your job well organized. If you can show your employer that the person who will replace you can slide into your role easily, that particular staff change will appear less costly.

Bad Timing

The promotion denial rationale of "bad timing" encompasses many reasons. Bad timing can be relevant to the financial season of the organization. If, say, you request a promotion-related raise during the organization's least financially rewarding time of the year, bad timing is a reasonable excuse for denying your promotion request. Or, bad timing may be attributed to your request's proximity to relevant office events. If, for instance, your promotion request takes place before an employee evaluation period or, worse, soon after you have received a less than glowing report, it appears that bad timing has affected your desire to receive a raise. Recent staff changes, a poor economy, holiday season's costliness, and your boss's bad day — many things can tag your request with the bad timing bug.

Bottom line: Take everything into account when you put together your plan for requesting a promotion. Just as many office happenings and time-of-year tendencies can hamper your ability to get the promotion you crave, you can use your understanding of interoffice mechanisms to your greatest advantage. Financial high season, post-positive review or personal coups, your boss's giddiness at being a first-time grandparent — surround your promotion request with all the goodness you can. If anything, let good timing affect your outcome.

The Employee's Attitude

Much of whether to bring an employee up in the organization is left to chance and opinion. That said, rejecting an employee's promotion based on perceptions of his or her attitude still says much about the person being denied a promotion. Throughout this book, a positive attitude has been mentioned as one of the top reasons employees get promoted. Not surprising, then, that the adverse is true: An employee's negatively perceived attitude can hold someone back from getting promoted. Top managers value employees who show tenacity, a strong work ethic, loyalty, an ability to work well with others, and eagerness associated with their job. They perceive demonstrations of these tendencies as being in line with having a positive attitude. Equally, those employees who whine, show up late, leave early, do not enjoy their job, cannot work in cooperation with others, and appear to lack motivation earn the "bad attitude" label and are less likely to be promoted.

Bottom line: Carry forth the duties of your job as if Big Brother is always watching. Enjoy the work you do, and treat every day as an opportunity to show what a valuable, positive employee you are. This does not mean you need to put on a façade and pretend as if you are the sunshine of the office. You do not have to affect your true personality to have a positive attitude. Having a positive attitude at work means treating your workplace, its employees, yourself, and the facets of your job with respect. You are being paid to do a job, and that job is providing you with opportunities for growth every day you come to work. So why not do your best? Be noticed for your positive attitude.

No Room for Growth

Especially in smaller organizations, at times there is simply no room for entry into another position in relation to your promotion. If everyone above you is content in their positions or few positions exist at levels above you in which you could rise in the company, you may not have a viable opportunity to earn a higher-level spot according to your present desires for professional growth. In some cases, the promotion denial reason that the organization does not have room for growth may be attributed to the perception that, although the promotion-requesting employee demonstrates potential, the gap between her present position and the next available position up is too expansive. At other times, the "no room for growth" defense could be, quite simply, an easy excuse. Even if the employee who is requesting access to a higher position is a valuable team member, the easiest course of action for an employer is often no action.

Bottom line: Whether there are no immediately viable upward options or it is just a convenient excuse, the "no room for growth" defense is a flimsy one that can be combatted fairly easily. If there are no open positions, the next-level position is a huge leap from your present one or you have reason to believe that your employer just is not motivated yet to commit to your rise up, get creative in offering a solution to the conundrum. For instance, ask for added responsibilities to your present workload. This, in essence, can create a new position or, at least, provides a middle ground segue into the higher-level positions.

Or, more boldly, suggest a new position (based on your researched assessment of the organization) that would contribute to your professional growth as well as the needs of the company.

Too Much Competition

Competition for workplace positions is stiffer than ever before. This influx in competitiveness makes sense if you look at the makeup of the present-day workforce dynamics. Today, employees are more likely to be college educated or have specialized training certification; have access to a global, broad base of information through the Internet; believe that they are entitled to success and, thus, are more likely to attain it; and tend toward work-centered lifestyles. Some of these "improvements" in work culture could be perceived to be detriments as in the case of focusing all one's time and energy to work-related growth at the expense of personal growth. However, because the individuals who make up today's workforce are all more likely to have marketable traits, the playing field is, in a way, leveled. So, although you may have an amazing résumé and the work ethic to match, there may be many coworkers and potential new hires who match your skill set, and this stark competition may be the biggest hurdle in your path.

Bottom line: In the ambiguous competition of workforce growth, your best bet is to focus on your own situation and not the intimidating coworker breathing down your neck for the same position. Do not get caught up in trying to tear that person down or scheming to make him or her look bad. Stay true to your work ethic, keep learning, stay positive, and always do your best work. In a sea of similarly trained and valuable employees, your best bet is to stand out in the crowd for the fine personal attributes that your peers forgot to hone while they were busy "just doing the job" in an effort to appear the most productive. Although production matters, it is the whole person who gets promoted, not just her productivity records.

Not a Team Player

The inability to work well with others is another common reason for not promoting workers and one that does not bode well for the individual's capacity as a team player. In kindergarten, a huge component of the whole year's curriculum is learning how to play well with others. Yet, even into adulthood, the concept is still not easily grasped or, at least, applied. Multiple factors can contribute to the perception or reality that an individual is not a team player. Some employees simply do not get along with other people, sometimes citing their individual work performance efficiency as reason enough not to work well in groups. However, top managers know that, for all the individual productivity in the world, to continue advancing through higher-level positions an individual will optimally be able to work effectively with others and demonstrate evidence of positive interpersonal skills.

Bottom line: A successfully functioning organization is much like a cohesive family unit, and Mom and Dad (your bosses) do not want to waste time mediating between the children. To eliminate the potential label that you are "not a team player" you must find a way to work well with others, even those who drive you a little crazy. In your work family you may have the crazy but well-meaning aunt, the loud-mouthed brother-in-law whose bawdy sense of humor will sometimes offend, and the cousin whose specialty is taming others' conflicts but who neglects her own. But, just like your family, you can find a way to accept them all. Being a good team player relies on one's ability to recognize each family member's individual strengths and dysfunctions to unearth the best working relationship between all members for the good of the family.

Limited Evidence of Productivity

Unless the post you currently hold is associated with some sort of record of productivity, as might be the case in a sales position or a position in which you are directly responsible for bringing funds into the organization, your employer may be forced to rely on a vague gauge to determine your level of productivity. If you do not make yourself stand out as a major workplace contributor, the conclusion your boss will come to is that you are not a major workplace contributor. In the absence of any established system to produce evidence of productivity, an employer has no choice but to work from his or her own presumptions of productivity. Thus, if it comes down to determining whether you are productive enough to warrant giving you more responsibility related to a promotion, based on a lack of evidence suggesting otherwise, he or she will defer to the easy conclusion that you are not necessarily productive enough in the position you already hold.

Bottom line: Because no one else has any motivation to do so, sometimes you have to toot your own horn. If you accomplish something good at work, be proud of it and exude that pride to your boss. You do not have to resort to obnoxious boastfulness to point out that you have contributed to the good of the organization. Do not be afraid to head into your boss's office and excitedly relay your recent good news. Not only will it make your boss's day to hear good news for the company, but you will look good in his or her eyes for sharing pertinent information, being excited for your contribution, and showing her that you are a good contributor.

Just Not Right for the Requested Position

Assuming that the position you are requesting to be promoted into is related to the work you already do, the rationale that you are "just not right for the position" can be interpreted to mean any number of things. It could mean your skill set is deemed unqualified for the role. Perhaps the suggestion is that, although your current position requires minimal customer contact, your employer feels the position you want requires more customer service than you are known to be prepared to handle. Or, maybe, she might see you as a stellar assistant and the position you desire requires leadership skills that you have not yet had the opportunity to demonstrate to full capacity. Being deemed "just not right for the position" could even simply mean your boss does not like you personally. Obviously, this is reason enough for her not to want to bring you closer up to her level. Then, of course, it may be that you are just not right for the position you desire. Possibly, the position you are in is different enough from the position you desire to suggest an ill fit. Or, you have a deficit in your skill set that, at this point, does not qualify you as the best one for the job.

Bottom line: Because you are a malleable human being, there is no reason you should be determined to be "just not right for the position." Find out the exact responsibilities of and skill set required for the position you desire so you may work on any potential, workable deficiencies you might have. You may not have the opportunity in your current position to demonstrate you are the right person for the job, so you may have to create ways to highlight those hidden talents or skills you have worked to improve. If, for example, high-level writing skills are requisite for the job you want but are not a component of your current position, find a way to show off your writing skills. For example, instead of telling your boss about your recent project, construct a well-written e-mail to exhibit your talents.

Excuses are like gallbladders. Everybody has one, but they do not do much except collect bile. If you have toned your workable deficiencies, drawn attention to your strengths, and counterargued the possibly problematic details of your promotion plan, there are no good excuses for absolute denial. Do not get stuck in the bile of excuses and stick with what you know to be true. Keep making consistent, genuine attempts toward your upward mobility in the organization, and you will succeed.

CHAPTER 14

What to Do After You Get the Promotion

You have worked so hard to get the promotion you want, and now that you have found success, your reward is more work. With your promotion, you will have more responsibility, new tasks, and heightened expectations to meet. Of course you are up to the challenge, but that does not remove from the fact that keeping up in a new position will take a new degree of effort. Now is not the time to get complacent after achieving your hard-fought victory. You have earned this opportunity, but with that achievement you also are faced with the understanding that you must deserve it and are obligated to continue to show your employer why you deserve it.

Lucky for you, though, going through these past 90 days of exercises in introspection has confirmed an extra hidden stash of energy in your favor. In today's society, it is simply too easy to fall in line with the speedy flow of the herd, to neglect yourself, and hide from problems. By honestly making consistent attempts at examining yourself and your work life, tending to your workable deficits, and creating ways to maximize your strengths, you have created a more refreshed, mindful, and efficient you. Like a good thorough physical at your doctor's office gives you direction on how to keep up your body, this process in complete personal introspection guarantees direction for upkeep in your professional life.

In the first 12 chapters you were presented with a collection of self-exploratory directives and, to explore the factors that affect your workplace experience. You applied these experiences in your promotion planning and implementation, but you are still benefiting from this self-examination and overhaul. In consulting an outside perspective (in this case, this book), you took the first step toward recognizing you needed assistance. The next step was applying the suggestions to better understand why, despite all attempts, you still were not confident that the promotion you desired would be yours. Finally, you put your plan into effect and got your promotion. You started from a point in which you needed to assess your equipment and conducted a complete overhaul. Fresh from that process, you have the momentum to propel yourself successfully through the next set of challenges related to your new position.

As you start this new position, apply all that you have learned from the first day in this position to begin with and maintain an ongoing, high level of competency. In your prior position you may have simply been keeping up with the demands of the job and, thus, failed to recognize all the instances in which you were sabotaging your chances for promotion by not going above the demands of the job. Now you can start this new position fresh, without your previous oversights. Apply the lessons you have learned, such as being mindful of your desires, thwarting the miswants that distract you, being proactive, practicing efficient organization, and effecting good communication. To use a car metaphor, you did the diagnostic and repair work; now it is all about maintenance.

Starting a new position is hard work. It is exciting and ripe for exhilarating new opportunities, but learning about the new tasks associated with the position, the deadlines, responsibilities, and everything else can be overwhelming when, during this learning process, you are expected to simultaneously tend to the demands of the new position. Understand that you must begin this new adventure on your own schedule and by the methods that will work most efficiently for you. You will be able to adapt to the position, learn everything, and perform extraordinarily in this new role. But as you are acclimating yourself into the position, take it easy and do not exceed the limitations of your personal learning curve. Now is the time to set up shop in exactly the manner that will benefit you in the long run.

If, with your promotion, you must move offices, consider the long-term structuring of your new office setting.

Apply the lessons from the chapter on organization and get everything set up specifically how it will work most beneficially for you. Organization of your office's elements for practical needs is only part of the picture, of course, because you will want also to design the environment of your office to benefit your need for comfort, too. You will be spending a good deal of your time in this setting, so the space must be comfortable and inviting to you and incorporate those calming effects to which you are partial. Take the time now to set everything up in the manner most conducive to your practical use and need for calm and comfort. As you get rolling in the job, you will be less likely to backtrack and tend to these self-serving aspects. But, as we have examined, you must take care of these simple needs to ensure your ongoing contentment.

Another aspect of your new position that you may need to devote time and energy to is going through the computer-based and hard-copy files that have been created through the history of your new position. You will want to acquaint yourself with this virtual and paper-based trail so you can learn as much as possible about the position to help yourself in the long run. History is the only thing we have to go on when planning for the future, so you must take the time to examine the history of your position. You will learn subtle details about your new job that no one would specifically think or even know to tell you about. You will learn about failures that could help you not to make the same mistakes as your predecessors. You will learn about successes that will help you as you attempt your own triumphs in the position. Set aside the time to do this research now so that when you get going in the position, you have an understanding of its history to help guide you.

Next, begin your placement in the job on the best foot by initiating the beginnings of your own trail, your upcoming brag sheet. As explained in Chapter 5, keeping an easily maintained brag sheet can be beneficial to the goals of keeping track of your accomplishments and providing a reference to the details of all that you have achieved. Even before you begin making strides in the position, get the document going so you can contribute to it efficiently as you move forward. One possible way to set up this document to benefit you in the long run is to separate sections in it according to the specific aspects of projects you will be completing. Analyze what you know about your position now so you can create an easy path toward memorializing your future contributions. For example, if your position consists of three different types of clients, organize your brag sheet now to separate those aspects into different sections. This way, when you start adding completed projects to your brag sheet, you will be able to do so in a much more organized format. This will serve you in the future, as you reflect back on your brag sheet, because you will be able to more quickly and efficiently locate the type of information you are attempting to reference.

In a new position, you will likely have a new pattern of time scheduling to consider. You may have just gotten a handle on controlling your time as it related to your last position, but now you must start fresh and try to figure out the pattern of your calendar all over again. Take a slow and careful look at the demands of your new position, the new to-dos you must factor in, the different responsibilities, tasks, and time-sensitive elements. Your goal is to plan your schedule in accommodation of all that you must accomplish but in a manner most conducive to allow for a pace and workload that will not overload you. Use the organization methods examined in Chapter 5 and plot out the pattern of your schedule now. Starting in this position fresh, you have the ability to control previous tendencies to do too much, spread yourself too thin, or end up feeling like you never have enough time. Remind yourself that those feelings of inadequacy and inefficiency were just an illusion. You can be productive and efficient without driving yourself crazy.

As you begin your new position, you will want to implant and further hone those systems you initiated before. By this point, you will have observed some of the benefits relevant to the establishment of the systems you have created and have a good idea of how you can improve them. Before you become entrenched in the duties and details of your new position, ensure you have a good working system of organization methods in place. These will assist you in the transition and for your long-term placement in the position. Fix what is not working and try new methods if you need more organization help. You will have a much easier time getting yourself organized now than if you were to do it as you become more involved in the responsibilities of the job.

CHAPTER 14: WHAT TO DO AFTER YOU GET THE PROMOTION

After you have tended to the tasks of preparing yourself, your office, and your understanding of the job so that you can move forward most efficiently, you are ready to begin tending to the job itself. Enter the role cautiously and open-mindedly. Do not assume that you will immediately adapt to the new responsibilities without hard work. You have your work and educational history behind you to back you up, but you are still in the process of learning the dynamics of this new position. Learn all there is to know about your job and keep up with what needs to get done. There is so much to learn now, but somewhere down the road you will have mastered this job as you did your last position.

In maintaining your success in this new role, you are doing half the work toward preparing for your next rise, and yet, there is always more planning to do to keep moving upward. Happy as you may be at earning rights to this new position, at some point you will max out that satisfaction. You will soon recognize a complacency that drove you to strive for your last promotion, and so it is then that you must begin your official promotion planning. In the meantime, however, you will be engaging in ongoing preparation for the next rise.

CHAPTER 15

Ongoing Preparation for the Next Rise

Pretend that today is the first day in your newly won role and you are ready to do everything right from the start to ensure your next transition up is a smooth one. This new role is an exciting one, but it is also a temporary appointment. This job will teach you many lessons and you will enjoy your accomplishments in the frame of it, but it is also likely a stepping stone to your next rise. This does not take away from the enjoyment of the moment. It is simply meant as a reminder to you of the power of upkeep and the urgency of avoiding complacency.

A huge part of doing a good job at work is found in enjoying what you do and taking pride in your successes and progress. When an individual has worked toward the goal of getting a promotion and has then been given access to a higher position in the organization, she or he will often slowly fall into a self-defeating trap: the tendency to become complacent.

Complacency can lead to a particular type of false confidence. Complacent people can appear satisfied, content, and unbothered, but a potential for upcoming negativity of which these seemingly satisfied souls are not aware may be bubbling under the surface. Complacency, drawn out to its potential conclusion, can serve to simmer one's desires and may lead to the building of unconscious walls hiding a need for change.

You have worked hard to build up your career. Even before earning this promotion, you have invested hours of energy into this aspect of your life. Now, starting in this newly appointed role, you have been given a clean slate. Your ongoing success and progress is contingent on your ability to maintain your workload efficiently while still engaging in ongoing preparation for the next rise. Do not assume complacency with your current job is an ultimate goal. Always consider how you are using your present success and contentment as a continual step toward your future successes.

Because we are pretending that today is the first day of the rest of this job, start it off with full consideration of every aspect you have applied to win this position and get to this point in your life. Applying every lesson you learned from your past job and the process you involved yourself in to get your new job will be much easier than if you went back to old ways, just doing what it takes to get by and get the bare minimum done. Now, you recognize just how much goes into the consideration of promotable people.

Make this job your own and dissect every aspect of it to understand how you can best manage it. Figure out what skills you should work on and grow in the position. Further determine how to work with the pliable aspects of the position, such as personal organization, to devise methods that will best benefit you as you navigate through the job. Continue questioning yourself. How can you do a better job? How can you be more productive? How can you be more efficient?

In preparation for your next inevitable rise, begin your new job with application of the lessons you learned in the journey that got you to this point, the journey of working toward your promotion. Although you have plenty of aspects to your work life that should be considered, a good starting point is in paying attention to the upkeep of your qualifications, being mindful of those miswants that serve to distract and divert you, paying attention to potential for opportunities, and upkeep of your efforts toward effective communication and adherence to behaving with integrity.

You were qualified for your last position. You, ostensibly, are qualified to move into your new position. But, still, as times change and as you continue through the course of your new position, you will need to take steps to further advance your qualifications. In an ongoing effort to keep growing, learning, and preparing for your future, enlist the suggestions from Chapter 1 and find ways to learn new skills and hone your qualifications. Some of this work will be done on the job, as you acclimate yourself to the demands of this new position and rise to the challenge of meeting and exceeding those demands. In some cases, you will have to seek outside educational opportunities to prepare yourself for those challenges. To fully prepare yourself for this new position, the opportunities of your future, and the expectations of today's workforce climate, keep searching for means by which to learn and expand your skill set and qualifications.

Equally important to keeping your qualifications fresh is tending to your inner desires and weeding out those miswants that can send you down unnecessary and unproductive paths. Keep exploring what drives you to succeed, but do not get caught up in the confusion of misguided desires. Keep close tabs on what you want out of life and your work experiences. Delve into your specific desires. Follow their courses through inception and to completion. Exploring the origins of your desires and determining why you want what you want will diminish the likelihood for miswants to seep in and divert you from achieving what will make you most happy.

As you have learned, to locate the opportunities that will help you advance in your career and life, you must pay close attention to everything that is happening around you. Opportunities are not always so obvious, and sometimes you have to make them yourself. As you go about tending to the details and demands of this new position, pay careful attention to what might be a potential opportunity for your ongoing growth and advancement. Seize every opportunity you detect. As you may recall, the more attempts you make to achieve the more chances you create to achieve. Try 20 times and you may succeed once. But try 100 times and you have increased your odds of success five times over. Opportunities are everywhere. You simply need to seize them or create them.

Because communication is such a vital aspect of all that drives connectivity between people and the current of the workplace, you must continue paying attention to the effectiveness of yours. Keep up with those aspects of communication that you do well, but pay special attention to the aspects that intimidate you. Practice what causes you the most trouble. If written communication, for example, is your trouble spot, take the time to initiate some group e-mails communicating details of what you have contributed to shared projects. As you continue your efforts toward moving up in the organization, upper management will be looking for those individuals who are well rounded and can adapt to the higher-level needs of the top-tiered positions. Being able to effectively communicate in all manners is a certain sign of well roundedness.

Having re-examined your sense and expression of the personal integrity you should enact on a day-to-day basis, continue supplanting those high standards in all stretches of how you conduct yourself in the workplace. You have been able to get the promotion you want through virtuous means. Stay true to your morals and keep engaging in those behaviors that are in line with acting with integrity. This will serve you positively as you advance in your career and will ensure that you can be confident you are making good decisions. Always remember, good guys do not finish last, so there is no reason to resort to bad behavior.

Preparing now for your eventual rise to the next stage of your career makes good sense. You can certainly meet and exceed the demands of your current position while taking steps to ensure that when the time comes to move forward you will be ready. Keep paying attention to the lessons and opportunities all around you, and gear up for your next rise.

Conclusion

Congratulations on your success. Whatever strides you have made in your personal and work lives are completely attributable to the work and painstaking introspection you have worked so hard at these past few months. It is rarely easy to take that long, hard look in the mirror and make the changes necessary to grow, but it is always beneficial.

The work you have put in now will continue to bring you rewards as you continue on through your journey in your career and in life. Just when you think you have taken all you can from the lessons you have learned, you will determine new ways to build on what you have discovered during this process. You will uncover new means to keep growing, learning, and advancing. If you keep paying attention to the world around you and your place in it, you will keep finding opportunities to enrich your improvement.

I hope that this book has functioned as a helpful friend would, to be by your side along the way and encourage you to consider the multitude of ways in which we can all improve ourselves. We are all works in progress, after all, and sometimes, to rediscover the means by which we can keep progressing, all it takes is another, different perspective. Or, as in the case of this particular book, it takes the perspectives of multiple top hiring managers, professionals, and workplace experts.

Your success is all your own, of course, because you are the one who took the time to explore deep within yourself and come up with the personal reasons you had been looked over in the past. You did all the work of becoming a more efficient worker, a more productive employee, a better candidate for the position you wanted now, and for the potential positions you may build to in the future.

As you continue forward in your career, remember the introspection of these past weeks and persist in application of those ideas that have been most meaningful to you. Tend to the upkeep of who you are in the workplace, the goals that drive you, the miswants that distract you, the opportunities available to you, the manner in which you communicate and maintain your integrity, the relationships and network you are building, and all the other lessons in which you have engaged. If you pay attention to the ideas that have contributed to your learning and the achievement of your goals and you continue to seek more life lessons from here forward, you will continue to improve, learn, grow, and move forward at work. In this way, you will never grow stagnant and dissatisfied in your job. You will keep progressing at work and in life.

At the start of this book, the overwhelming dissatisfaction of the working population at large was put into perspective. You began this journey in familiarity with the roughly 85 percent of these people who claimed dissatisfaction. Perhaps you, too, felt voiceless and unimportant at work. But you soon learned that you could overcome that dissatisfaction, that all you had to do was speak up so you could be heard and be recognized as the valuable employee you knew you could become all along. Instead of resigning yourself to spending thousands of hours each year amid the grime and discomfort of taking a siesta on your lawn, you sought out the better option of a cushy cot indoors. You had to do the work to create that more comfortable environment but all the better to now enjoy it.

Keep up the hard work of self-directed mindfulness, and stay true to the goals you have set for yourself. Success will always be yours if you continue building on this platform of ongoing growth and self-exploration.

Bibliography

Asher, Donald. *Who Gets Promoted, Who Doesn't, and Why: 10 Things You'd Better Do if you Want to Get Ahead.* Ten Speed Press, Berkeley, CA (2007).

Bernthal, Paul. "A survey of trust in the workplace: An executive summary." Development Dimensions International, 1993.

Borenstein, Seth. "Harvard study: Nice guys actually finish first." *USA Today*. March 19, 2008.

Buckingham, Marcus. *Go Put Your Strengths to Work: 6 Powerful Steps to Achieve Outstanding Performance.* Free Press, New York (2007).

Chambers, Harry E. *Getting Promoted: Real Strategies for Advancing Your Career.* Perseus Books, New York (1999).

Duhachek, Adam, Shuoyang Zhang, and Shanker Krishnan. "Anticipated Group Interaction: Valence Asymmetries in Attitude Shift." *Journal of Consumer Research*. 2007.

Freeman, Richard B. and Joel Rogers. *What Workers Want.* Cornell University Press, Ithaca, NY (1999).

Friedman, Lynn. "When You Are Denied a Promotion." *The Washington Post.* November 23, 2005.

Irvine, William B. *On Desire: Why We Want What We Want.* Oxford University Press, Oxford, England (2007).

Karseras, Hugh. *From New Recruit to High Flyer.* Kogan Page, London. (2006).

Peter, Laurence J. and Raymond Hull. *The Peter Principle.* Bantam Books, New York (1970).

Shambaugh, Rebecca. *It's Not the Glass Ceiling, It's the Sticky Floor.* McGraw-Hill, New York (2007).

Tracy, Brian. *Get Paid More and Promoted Faster: 21 Great Ways to Get Ahead in Your Career.* Berrett-Kpehler Publishers, San Francisco (2001).

Whitcomb, Susan Britton. *30-Day Job Promotion: Build a Powerful Promotion Plan in a Month.* Jist Works, Indianapolis, Indiana (2008).

"What's the best day to ask for a raise?" *New Mexico Business Journal.* March 2000.

Author Biography

Lexi M. Schuh lives in Denver, Colorado, with her husband and three children. In addition to her research in career development, Lexi writes on a variety of other topics and has had her work included in numerous publications such as *The Healthy Planet*, a natural living publication, and *bizMe*, a periodical workplace guide for women.

Index

A

Accessories, 126, 134

Achievement, 255, 58, 270, 279, 17

Appearance, 228-229, 235-236, 238, 117, 126-129, 279, 9

Attitude, 273, 28-29, 32, 40, 234, 247-248, 79, 81, 88-91, 123, 164, 169, 176-179, 6, 9

B

Bad Timing, 246-247, 9

Balance, 45, 47-50, 53, 61, 158, 5

Boss, 29, 34, 39, 202, 208, 210, 217-218, 228-232, 234-236, 238, 241-242, 244, 247, 252-254, 53-56, 63, 65-67, 70, 75-76, 80-83, 86, 93-95, 109, 132-133, 145-148, 153-156, 158-167, 169-185, 11, 279, 20, 6, 8

Budget, 244-245, 279, 9

C

Case, 34, 39, 191, 195, 208, 214, 220, 230-233, 235, 249, 251, 256, 52, 58, 73, 87-89, 104, 110, 112-113,

132-133, 135, 148, 151-153, 155-157, 159, 164, 167, 177, 270, 279, 18, 7

Character, 193, 196, 205, 207, 222-225, 233, 119, 170-171, 178, 9

Clothing, 227, 236, 239, 128, 134, 147

Communication, 36, 189, 191-192, 196-197, 214, 228-229, 232-233, 239, 257, 265, 267, 56, 129, 131-149, 173, 176-177, 279, 7

Company, 32, 208, 211, 218, 244, 248-249, 252, 45, 50, 52, 65, 70-71, 84-85, 91, 93, 95-96, 144, 152, 163, 165-166, 175, 279, 286, 6

Competition, 31-33, 249-250, 113, 118, 279, 9

Conflict Management, 187, 190-191, 193, 214, 8

Context, 231, 234, 59, 84, 120, 128, 131-132, 144, 149, 7

Conversation, 229, 232-234, 131, 136, 138, 173, 9

Counterarguments, 235, 92, 162-163, 7

Coworker, 188, 231, 250, 75, 107, 111, 117, 132-133, 145, 279

Current Role, 27, 5

Customer Service, 36, 205, 208, 213-215, 253, 135, 141, 9

D

Dedication, 81, 91-92, 279, 4, 6

Denied, 274, 239, 241, 247, 162, 279, 19, 9

Dependability, 205-206, 215, 217, 9

Duties, 29, 36, 38, 248, 260, 48, 51-52, 81-82, 100, 103, 111-112, 11, 279, 19-20, 7

E

Education, 37-38, 51, 58, 61, 64, 81, 83-84, 87-88, 97, 141, 159, 279, 6

Employee, 28, 37, 193, 218-219, 225, 231, 236, 241, 245-249, 43, 54-55, 60, 65, 67, 73, 76, 80, 84, 87, 91, 95, 131-133, 145, 154, 156, 171, 174, 176-177, 181-182, 270-271, 11-13, 279, 15-16, 20-21, 9

Employer, 24-25, 245-246, 249, 252-253, 255, 49, 60, 70, 87, 92, 96-97, 144, 146, 148, 167, 279, 20

Entitlement, 24, 26, 32, 41, 218, 74, 97, 152, 5

Expectations, 24, 213-214, 255, 266, 81, 92, 151, 157, 160, 162, 164-165, 8

Experience, 25, 29, 193, 199, 202, 208, 240, 256, 43, 58, 64, 71, 122-123, 136-137, 153, 161, 170, 172, 180, 184, 11-13, 279, 15, 17

F

Field, 24, 31, 37-38, 199, 238, 250, 43, 50, 52, 62, 84, 86, 89, 158, 279, 5-6

G

Goal, 190, 192, 209, 212, 215, 220, 239, 241, 245, 259, 263-264, 45, 53, 55-62, 87, 96, 101, 111, 139, 153, 159, 164, 174-175, 177, 180, 17-18, 20-21

Growth, 25, 36-37, 40, 194, 239, 242, 248-250, 266, 54, 60, 64-65, 67-68, 70, 76, 97, 129, 171, 177, 271, 19-20, 22, 9

H

Hire, 12-13

Honesty, 206-213, 219, 225, 8

I

Integrity, 203, 205-210, 213-214, 218-219, 222-224, 265, 267, 270, 19, 8

J

Job, 274, 24, 26-27, 29, 31-32, 35-40, 195, 198, 204, 213-214, 216-217, 219, 236, 242, 246-248, 250, 253, 256-258, 260-261, 263-265, 43, 45, 49, 52-55, 58, 62, 64, 67, 69, 76, 79-84, 87, 90-93, 95-97, 100, 103, 107, 111-113, 123, 132-133, 147-148, 152, 154-155, 159, 161-164, 175-176, 179-181, 185, 270, 11-12, 15-17, 19-22, 6

L

Language, 141, 174

Leadership, 198-199, 208, 253, 169, 178-180

Loyalty, 206, 218-219, 247, 9

M

Manager, 195, 208, 88, 167, 175, 11-13, 2

Meeting, 200, 227-228, 230-239, 244-245, 266, 59, 63, 86, 103, 127, 145, 153-156, 161, 165-167, 181-184, 19, 8

Mentor, 200-201, 170

Messages, 129, 131-134, 136, 144-146, 148-149, 7

Miswanting, 45-46, 5

N

Needs, 25, 27, 201, 208, 216-217, 219, 249, 257-258, 260, 267, 49, 51, 54, 58, 65, 68, 85, 93-94, 99-103, 105,

107, 109, 111, 113, 115, 141, 176, 178, 11, 17, 6

Negativity, 202-203, 210, 264, 89-91

Networking, 187, 190, 199-200, 48, 68, 84-86, 8

O

Office, 29, 31, 34, 187-190, 193-194, 196, 199, 202-205, 216-217, 236-237, 246-248, 252, 256-258, 260, 43, 54, 63-64, 66, 68, 71, 90, 92-94, 99, 106, 108, 110-111, 113-114, 122, 128, 142-143, 145-146, 163, 170, 175-178, 3, 5, 8

Office Politics, 187-188, 190, 202-204, 54, 176, 8

Opportunity, 30, 36, 38, 41, 189-190, 198, 203-204, 208, 210-211, 224, 228-229, 232, 234, 236, 239, 242, 246, 248, 253, 255, 266, 55, 64, 66-71, 75-76, 79-80, 85, 87, 90, 96-97, 144, 149, 158, 163, 169, 181, 185, 17, 20

Organize, 259, 58, 106, 110-111

P

Pay, 30-31, 33-34, 36, 189, 211, 237, 244-245, 266-267, 49, 55, 76, 86, 97, 131, 144, 146, 148-149, 159, 169, 172-174, 183, 270, 20

Peer, 192, 84

Performance, 273, 244, 251, 76, 79-81, 95, 152-153, 158, 11-12, 20, 6

Practice, 24, 29, 38, 187, 227-228, 231-232, 235, 240, 267, 43, 84, 97, 109, 119, 122, 138, 140, 149, 156, 180, 19, 9

Preparation, 228, 230, 233, 261, 263-265, 155-157, 7, 9-10

Presentation, 228, 231-232, 235, 238, 240, 91, 117-118, 127, 146-147, 153, 155-157, 164, 7

Proactive, 29, 257, 64, 71, 73-76, 11, 6

Productivity, 204, 244, 250-252, 55, 71, 79, 81, 83, 89, 91, 93, 104, 152, 169, 180, 183, 10

Project, 194, 216, 254, 69, 96, 99, 112, 132-133, 148, 155, 158

Protocol, 244, 43-44, 141, 166, 9

R

Relationships, 26-27, 189-190, 193-199, 202, 204, 48, 74, 102, 148, 177, 184, 270, 8

Reputation, 29-30, 205, 207, 217, 222-224, 123, 5, 9

Request, 230, 244, 246-247, 107, 122, 143, 153, 157, 159-160, 162, 164, 169, 171, 174

S

Scheduling, 259, 165, 167, 8

Sincerity, 206, 219-221, 9

Staff Changes, 245-246, 9

Strength, 35, 215, 66, 17

Stress, 229, 234, 236, 87, 100, 104, 107, 113-115

Structure, 109, 156

Supervisor, 189, 165, 167, 169, 11

Synopses, 111, 7

T

Team Player, 250-251, 10

INDEX

Time Management, 104-105, 107, 113, 6

Timing, 246-247, 166, 9

Trust, 273, 205, 211-212, 225, 85, 123, 176, 13, 3, 8

W

Work, 273, 275, 23-30, 32, 34-38, 40, 187-193, 195-199, 201, 203-206, 209, 212-213, 216, 218, 223-225, 227-233, 236, 239, 242-243, 245, 247-253, 255-257, 260-261, 263, 265-266, 43-45, 47-55, 57-59, 61-62, 64-65, 67, 70, 72-73, 76, 79-97, 99-115, 117-120, 126-127, 132-133, 139, 142-143, 146, 148-149, 152-156, 158-159, 161-162, 164-166, 170-173, 175-176, 178-181, 269-271, 11-13, 15-18, 20-22, 2-3, 5

Workforce, 23-26, 31, 40, 211, 244, 249-250, 266, 58-59, 92, 16-17, 5

Workplace, 273, 275, 23-27, 32, 40-41, 193-194, 198, 203-204, 207, 211-214, 216, 237, 244, 248-249, 252, 256, 267, 44, 51, 53, 55, 63, 67, 69, 72-74, 80-81, 88-89, 94, 100, 104-105, 113-114, 117, 120-121, 123-124, 126, 129, 139-142, 144, 147, 149, 152, 154-155, 163, 166, 170-171, 173-176, 178-179, 270, 12-13, 15, 20

Writing, 38, 253, 139-141, 143, 7

DID YOU BORROW THIS COPY?

Have you been borrowing a copy of *How to Get the Promotion You Want in 90 Days or Less: A Step-by-Step Plan for Making It Happen* from a friend, colleague or library? Wouldn't you like your own copy for quick and easy reference? To order, photocopy the form below and send to:

Atlantic Publishing Company
1405 SW 6th Ave • Ocala, FL 34471

YES!

Send me ____ copy(ies) of *How to Get the Promotion You Want in 90 Days or Less: A Step-by-Step Plan for Making It Happen* for $24.95 plus $7.00 for shipping and handling.

Please Print

_____
Name

_____
Organization Name

_____
Address

_____
City, State, Zip

❏ My check or money order is enclosed. *Please make checks payable to Atlantic Publishing Company.*

❏ My purchase order is attached. *PO #* _____

www.atlantic-pub.com • e-mail: sales@atlantic-pub.com

Order toll-free 800-814-1132
FAX 352-622-1875

Atlantic Publishing Company
1405 SW 6th Ave • Ocala, FL 34471

Add $7.00 for USPS shipping and handling. For Florida residents PLEASE add the appropriate sales tax for your county.